LONGMAN

Photo Dictionary
of American English

W9-BXZ-465

PEARSON
Longman

www.longman.com

NEW EDITION

CONTENTS

CONTENTS

1 one
2 two
3 three
4 four
5 five
6 six
7 seven
8 eight
9 nine

10 ten
11 eleven
12 twelve
13 thirteen
14 fourteen
15 fifteen
16 sixteen
17 seventeen
18 eighteen

19 nineteen
20 twenty
21 twenty-one
30 thirty
40 forty
50 fifty
60 sixty
70 seventy
80 eighty

90 ninety
100 one hundred

× times/multiplied by

— minus

÷ divided by

+ plus

= equals

101 one hundred and one

1,000 one thousand

10,000 ten thousand

100,000 one-hundred thousand

1,000,000 one million

100% — **100** one hundred percent
— **90**
— **80**
— **70**
— **60**
50% — **50** fifty percent
— **40**
— **30**
20% — **20** twenty percent
10% — **10** ten percent
— **0** zero percent

1 first
2 second
3 third
4 fourth
5 fifth

A CUBE

1 height
2 corner
3 top
4 depth
5 edge
6 face

B ISOSCELES TRIANGLE

7 obtuse angle
8 acute angle

C RIGHT TRIANGLE

9 apex
10 hypotenuse
11 right angle
12 base

D SQUARE

13 side

E RECTANGLE

14 length
15 diagonal
16 width

F CIRCLE

17 circumference
18 center
19 diameter
20 radius

G OVAL/ELLIPSE

H CYLINDER

I SPHERE

J LINES

21 perpendicular
22 straight
23 parallel
24 spiral

Discussion

1 Give your partner instructions to draw a shape.
2 Find things that are shaped like a triangle, a square, a rectangle, and a cylinder.

A MONTHS

JANUARY	FEBRUARY	MARCH	APRIL	MAY	JUNE
S M T W T F S	S M T W T F S	S M T W T F S	S M T W T F S	S M T W T F S	S M T W T F S
1 2 3 4 5 6	1 2 3	1 2 3	1 2 3 4 5 6 7	1 2 3 4 5	1 2
7 8 9 10 11 12 13	4 5 6 7 8 9 10	4 5 6 7 8 9 10	8 9 10 11 12 13 14	6 7 8 9 10 11 12	3 4 5 6 7 8 9
14 15 16 17 18 19 20	11 12 13 14 15 16 17	11 12 13 14 15 16 17	15 16 17 18 19 20 21	13 14 15 16 17 18 19	10 11 12 13 14 15 16
21 22 23 24 25 26 27	18 19 20 21 22 23 24	18 19 20 21 22 23 24	22 23 24 25 26 27 28	20 21 22 23 24 25 26	17 18 19 20 21 22 23
28 29 30 31	25 26 27 28	25 26 27 28 29 30 31	29 30	27 28 29 30 31	24 25 26 27 28 29 30

JULY	AUGUST	SEPTEMBER	OCTOBER	NOVEMBER	DECEMBER
S M T W T F S	S M T W T F S	S M T W T F S	S M T W T F S	S M T W T F S	S M T W T F S
1 2 3 4 5 6 7	1 2 3 4	1	1 2 3 4 5 6	1 2 3	1
8 9 10 11 12 13 14	5 6 7 8 9 10 11	2 3 4 5 6 7 8	7 8 9 10 11 12 13	4 5 6 7 8 9 10	2 3 4 5 6 7 8
15 16 17 18 19 20 21	12 13 14 15 16 17 18	9 10 11 12 13 14 15	14 15 16 17 18 19 20	11 12 13 14 15 16 17	9 10 11 12 13 14 15
22 23 24 25 26 27 28	19 20 21 22 23 24 25	16 17 18 19 20 21 22	21 22 23 24 25 26 27	18 19 20 21 22 23 24	16 17 18 19 20 21 22
29 30 31	26 27 28 29 30 31	23 24 25 26 27 28 29	28 29 30 31	25 26 27 28 29 30	23 24 25 26 27 28 29
		30			30 31

B DAYS OF THE WEEK

October

Sunday	Monday	Tuesday	Wednesday	Thursday	Friday	Saturday
	1	2	3	4	5	6
7	8	9	10	11	12	13
14	15	16	17	18	19	
	22	23	24	25	26	
29	30	31				

C HOLIDAYS

1 Easter* (April)
2 Mother's Day* (May)
3 Memorial Day* (May)
4 Father's Day* (June)
5 Independence Day/Fourth of July (July 4th)
6 Halloween (October 31st)
7 Thanksgiving (Day)* (November)
8 Christmas (Day) (December 25th)
9 New Year's Eve (December 31st)
10 Valentine's Day (February 14th)

* the exact date changes from year to year

When's Valentine's Day?
It's on February fourteenth.

When's Christmas Day?
It's in December.

A: **When's Halloween?**
B: ....

A: **When's** .... ?
B: It's on (date)./It's in (month).

Discussion
1 Which of these are religious holidays?
2 Which holidays do you celebrate in your own country? When are they?

1 clock
2 hour hand
3 minute hand
4 second hand
5 face
6 (digital) watch
7 (analog) watch
8 twelve o'clock (midnight)
9 twelve o'clock (noon/midday)
10 seven (o'clock)
11 seven oh five/five after seven
12 seven ten/ten after seven
13 seven fifteen/(a) quarter after seven
14 seven twenty/twenty after seven
15 seven thirty

 12:00
 7:00
 7:05
 7:10
 7:15
 7:20

 7:30
 7:35
 7:40
 7:45
 7:50

 7:55
 8:00

16 seven thirty-five/twenty-five to eight
17 seven forty/twenty to eight
18 seven forty-five/(a) quarter to eight
19 seven fifty/ten to eight
20 seven fifty-five/five to eight
21 eight a.m./eight (o'clock) in the morning
22 eight p.m./eight (o'clock) in the evening

What time is it?
It's ten ten./It is ten after ten.

A: What time is it?
B: It is ....

Discussion
1 What time is it?
2 What time do you get up/ go to bed?

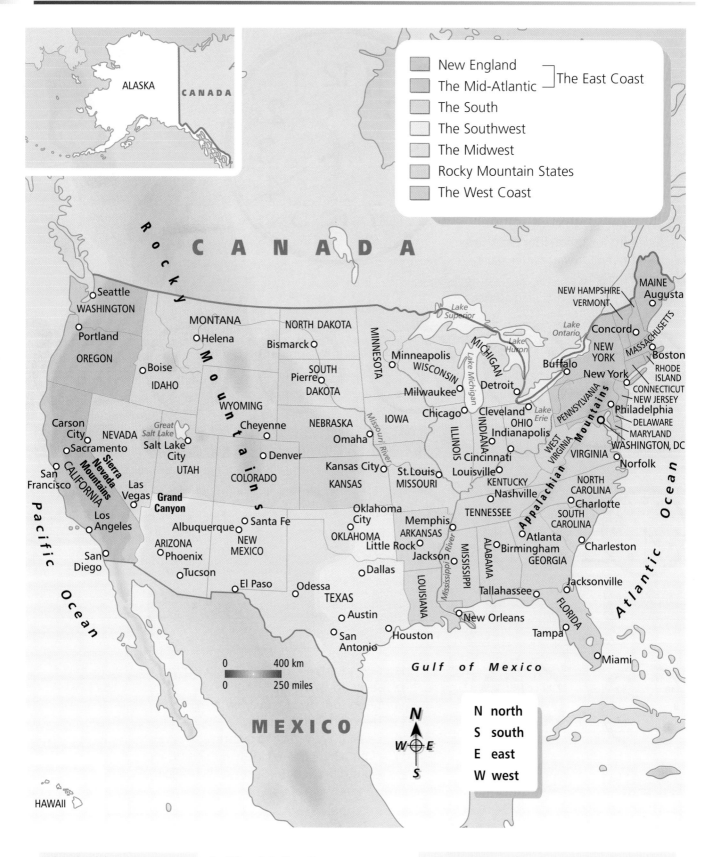

New England ⎤
The Mid-Atlantic ⎦ The East Coast
The South
The Southwest
The Midwest
Rocky Mountain States
The West Coast

Where's Alabama?
It's east of Mississippi and west of Georgia.

Where's Kansas?
It's south of Nebraska and north of Oklahoma.

A: **Where's Indiana?**
B: It's ....

A: **Where's** ....?
B: It's .... of ....
and .... of ....

Discussion

1 Which states are on the Atlantic Ocean? the Pacific Ocean? the Gulf of Mexico?

2 Which states are next to Canada? Mexico?

Application Form

Please complete all of the items on this form. Use blue or black ink only.

Application for .Design Manager.........

Last/Family Name .Edwards............

First Name ......Susan............ Middle Initial ......C.

Date of Birth .04/24/66. Place of Birth .New York.........

Country of Birth ..USA.........

Emergency Contact .Paul Edwards.............

Address .734 Center Drive, Suite 103......

..........La Mesa, California.........

..........USA.........

..........Zip Code .91652..........

E-Mail Address .susan.edwards@uol.com........

Previous Employment ....

.Hart Design, New York 1998–present.......

.JPB Design Associates 1993–1998.......

1 single
2 couple
3 married
4 divorced

5 widow
6 widower
7 girl
8 boy
9 baby
10 child
11 toddler
12 man
13 woman
14 teenager
15 adult
16 senior citizen

What's your address?
It's 63 Maple Street.

What's your marital status?
I'm married./I'm a widow.

A: **What's your marital status?**
B: I'm ....

A: **What's your** .... ?
B: It's/I'm (a) ....

Discussion
1 Give the personal data of someone you know.
2 Give the personal data of a famous person.

A MARRIED COUPLE
1 husband
2 wife
3 ex-husband
4 ex-wife

B PARENTS AND CHILDREN
5 father
6 mother
7 daughter
8 son

C GRANDPARENTS AND GRANDCHILDREN
9 grandfather
10 grandmother
11 granddaughter
12 grandson

D SIBLINGS
13 sister
14 brother

Who's she?
She's Julia's mother.

Who's he?
He's Tom's son.

A: **Who's she?**
B: ....

A: **Who's he/she?**
B: He/She's .... 's
....

Discussion
1 Which of these words can be used only for women? only for men? both men and women?
2 Draw your family tree and describe it.

E

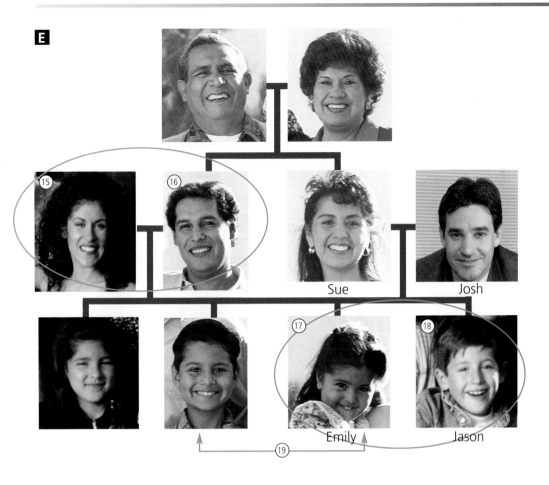

Sue   Josh

Emily   Jason

E OTHER RELATIVES

15 aunt
16 uncle
17 niece
18 nephew
19 cousins

F

F IN-LAWS

20 father-in-law
21 mother-in-law
22 daughter-in-law
23 son-in-law
24 sister-in-law
25 brother-in-law

2.3 DAILY ROUTINE/HOME ACTIVITIES

1 wake up
2 get up
3 wash your face
4 rinse your face
5 dry your face/yourself
6 brush your teeth
7 take a shower
8 shave
9 get dressed
10 comb your hair
11 put on make-up
12 eat breakfast
13 have a cup of coffee
14 go to work

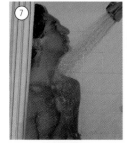

15 watch (TV)
16 read (the paper)
17 listen to the radio
18 take a bath
19 brush your hair
20 go to bed
21 sleep

Is she getting up?
Yes, she is.

Is he taking a shower?
No, he isn't. He's watching TV.

A: **Is she listening to the radio?**
B: ....

A: **Is he/she .... ?**
B: Yes, he/she is./No, he/she isn't.

Discussion

1 Which of these things do you do in the morning? In what order?

2 Which of these things do you do in the evening? In what order?

12

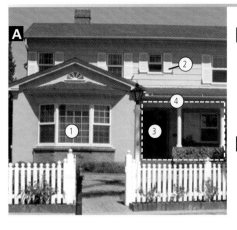

A HOUSE
1 window
2 shutter
3 (front) door
4 (front) porch

B DUPLEX
5 (front) yard
6 walkway
7 screen door

C RANCH HOUSE
8 gutter
9 drainpipe
10 fence
11 driveway
12 roof
13 mailbox
14 garage
15 chimney
16 satellite dish
17 TV antenna

D FRONT DOOR
18 knocker
19 doorbell
20 intercom
21 doorknob

E TOWNHOUSE

F APARTMENT BUILDING
22 fire escape
23 balcony

Does this house have a front porch?
No, it doesn't.

Does this house have a chimney?
Yes, it does.

A: Does this house have a(n)
.... ?

B: Yes it does./No, it doesn't.

A: Does this .... have a(n)
.... ?

B: Yes, it does./No, it doesn't.

Discussion
1 What kinds of places to live are there in your city?
2 Where do you live? Describe your home.

1 freezer
2 refrigerator
3 faucet
4 counter/counter top
5 sink
6 cupboard/cabinet
7 stove
8 oven
9 burner
10 dishwasher
11 microwave (oven)

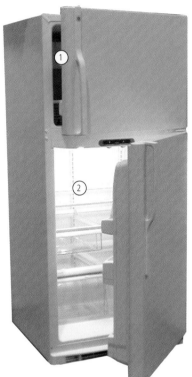

12 cookbook
13 storage jar
14 spices
15 spice rack
16 dishwashing liquid
17 scouring pad
18 trash can/garbage can

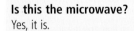

Is this the microwave?
Yes, it is.

Is this the stove?
No, it isn't. It's the oven.

A: **Is this the** .... ?
B: Yes, it is./No, it isn't. It's the
....

Discussion

1 Which of these things do you have in your kitchen?

2 Which of these things do you need?

1 wok
2 ladle
3 pot
4 toaster
5 pot holder
6 cookie sheet
7 egg beaters
8 tea kettle
9 knife
10 cutting board
11 food processor
12 roasting pan
13 blender
14 peeler
15 garlic press
16 can opener
17 rolling pin
18 sieve
19 colander
20 steamer

21	measuring spoons	27	bottle opener
22	grater	28	coffee maker
23	(mixing) bowl	29	handle
24	whisk	30	saucepan
25	measuring cup	31	lid
26	(electric) mixer	32	frying pan

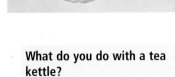

What do you do with a tea kettle?
You boil water in it.

What do you do with a wok?
You stir-fry vegetables in it.

A: **What do you do with a(n)**
.... ?
B: You ....
in/ with it.

Discussion
1 Which of these things do you have in your kitchen?
2 Which things would you like to have? Why?

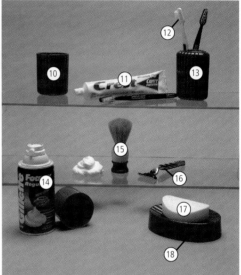

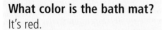
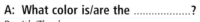

1 shower
2 shower curtain
3 mirror
4 shelf
5 bathtub
6 tile
7 toilet
8 bath mat
9 laundry basket/hamper

10 cup
11 toothpaste
12 toothbrush
13 toothbrush holder
14 shaving cream
15 shaving brush
16 razor
17 soap
18 soap dish
19 medicine cabinet
20 towel rack
21 wash cloth
22 hand towel
23 bath towel
24 faucet
25 sink
26 toilet paper
27 box of tissues

What color is the bath mat?
It's red.

What color are the tiles?
They're white.

A: **What color is/are the ....?**
B: It's/They're ....

Discussion

1 Which of these things do you have in your bathroom? Which would you like to have?

2 Do you prefer taking a bath or a shower? Why?

1 curtains
2 lamp
3 nightstand/night table
4 double bed
5 bedspread
6 carpet
7 pillowcase
8 pillow
9 headboard
10 twin bed
11 quilt
12 wallpaper

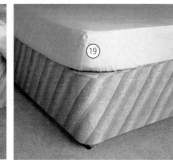

13 closet
14 dresser/chest of
   drawers
15 drawer
16 knob
17 comforter

18 (flat) sheet
19 (fitted) sheet
20 mirror
21 dressing table
22 alarm clock
23 mattress
24 dust ruffle

Where's the lamp?
It's on the nightstand.

Where's the bedskirt?
It's under the mattress.

A: **Where's the flat sheet?**
B: It's .... the ....

A: **Where's the** .... ?
B: It's on/under the ....

Discussion
1 What do you have in your bedroom?
2 Which of these things would you like to have?

17

7 (fireplace) screen	12 drape
8 planter	13 window
9 plant	14 coffee table
10 lamp	15 throw pillow
11 lampshade	16 cushion
	17 sofa/couch
	18 armchair
	19 furniture
	20 wall unit
	21 desk
	22 bookcase
	23 books

1 picture
2 picture frame
3 mantel(piece)
4 vase
5 flowers
6 fireplace

Where's the vase?
It's on the mantel.

Where are the books?
They're in the bookcase.

A: **Where's the lamp?**
B: It's .... the ....
A: **Where's/Where are the**
.... ?
B: It's/They're ....

Discussion
1 What do you have in your living room?
2 Do you like this living room? Why or why not?

1 sideboard
2 mirror
3 chandelier
4 (dining room) table
5 chair
6 teapot
7 pepper shaker
8 salt shaker
9 napkin
10 napkin ring
11 place mat
12 glass
13 pitcher

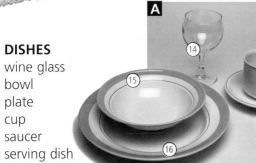

A DISHES

14 wine glass
15 bowl
16 plate
17 cup
18 saucer
19 serving dish

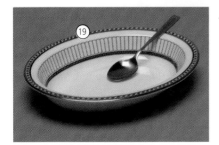

B SILVERWARE/CUTLERY

20 fork
21 knife
22 tablespoon
23 teaspoon

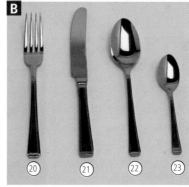

Where's the pepper?
It's to the left of the salt.

Where's the knife?
It's to the right of the fork.

A: Where's the .... ?
B: It's ....
   of the ....

Discussion

1 Which of these things are used for eating?
2 Which of these things do you use for drinking?

1 diaper
2 changing pad
3 potty chair
4 crib
5 stuffed animal
6 teddy bear
7 baby clothes
8 high chair
9 bib
10 pacifier
11 baby wipes
12 spill-proof cup
13 nipple
14 (baby) bottle
15 sterilizer

16 baby carriage
17 stroller
18 intercom/baby monitor
19 baby carrier
20 car seat

Where's the baby?
He's in his car seat.

Where's the baby?
She's in her crib.

A: **Where's the baby?**
B: He's/She's in/on his/her
....

Discussion
1 Which of these things are used for taking a baby outside?
2 Which of these things are used for feeding a baby?

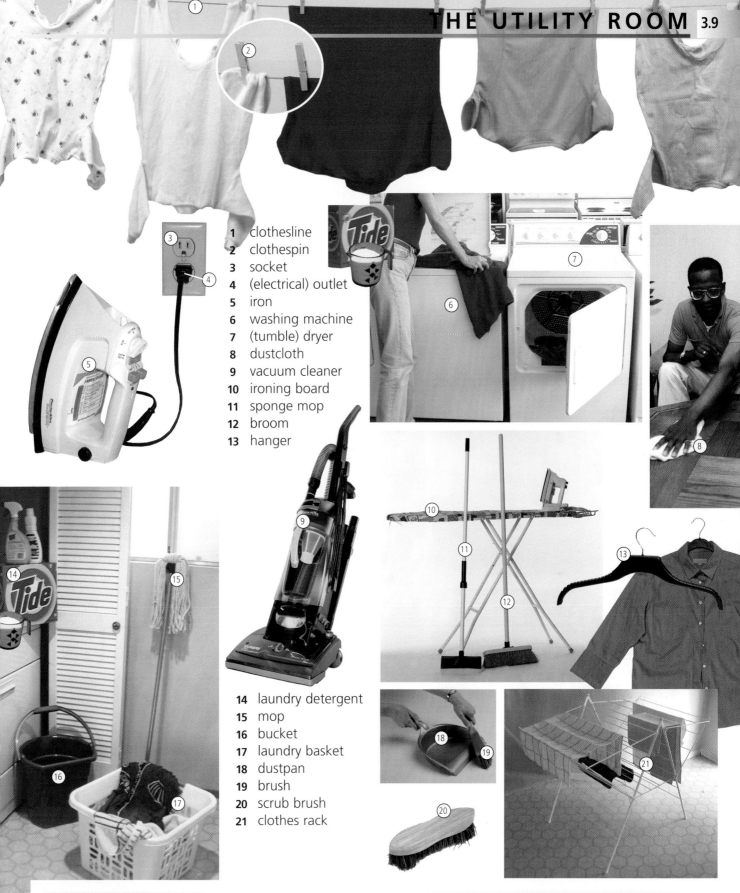

1 clothesline
2 clothespin
3 socket
4 (electrical) outlet
5 iron
6 washing machine
7 (tumble) dryer
8 dustcloth
9 vacuum cleaner
10 ironing board
11 sponge mop
12 broom
13 hanger

14 laundry detergent
15 mop
16 bucket
17 laundry basket
18 dustpan
19 brush
20 scrub brush
21 clothes rack

Where's the clothespin?
It's on the clothesline.

Where's the laundry?
It's in the laundry basket.

A: **Where's the laundry detergent?**
B: It's .... the ....

A: **Where's the .... ?**
B: It's in/on the ....

Discussion

1 Which of these things do you have in your home?

2 How often do you use these things?

1 umbrella
2 patio
3 (patio) table
4 (patio) chair
5 flowers
6 flowerbed
7 lawn
8 barbecue
9 yard
10 hedge
11 bush
12 tree
13 vegetable garden
14 lounge chair

15 daffodil
16 hyacinth
17 daisy
18 tulip
19 orchid
20 rose

Do you like roses?
Yes, I do.

Do you like hyacinths?
No, I don't.

A: **Do you like** .... ?
B: Yes, I do./No, I don't.

Discussion
1 Do you have a yard? a patio? Describe it.
2 Do you like to work with plants? What kind?

1 seeds
2 seedling tray
3 shed
4 compost
5 rake
6 fork
7 shovel/spade
8 planter
9 hose

10 wheelbarrow
11 watering can
12 garden shears
13 sprinkler

14 clippers
15 gardening gloves
16 trowel
17 lawn mower

ACTIONS

18 mow the lawn
19 plant flowers
20 rake (the) leaves
21 water the plants
22 dig the soil

A: I want to water the garden.
B: You need a watering can or a sprinkler.

A: I want to mow the lawn.
B: You need a lawn mower.

A: I want to ....
B: You need a(n) ....
and/or (a/an) ....

Discussion
1 Do you like gardening?
2 Which of these things do you do?

1 attic
2 second floor
3 staircase
4 bannister
5 hallway
6 first floor
7 stairs
8 basement/cellar

9 ceiling
10 window
11 window frame
12 window pane
13 screen
14 shutter
15 wall
16 floor

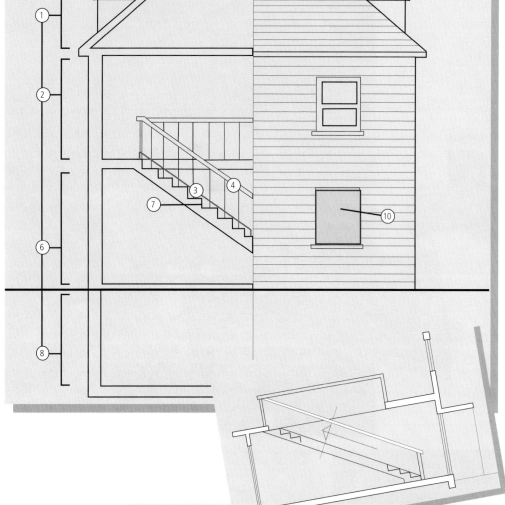

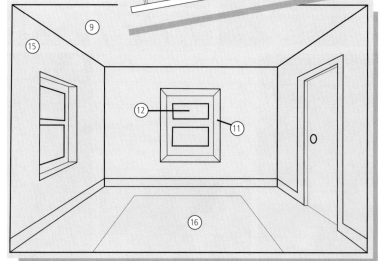

Does your home have a dining room?
No, it doesn't.

Does your home have stairs?
Yes, it does.

A: **Does your home have a(n)**
.... ?
B: Yes, it does./No, it doesn't.

Discussion
1 Which of these things do you have in your home?
2 Are there many two-story houses in your city?

1 make the bed
2 make breakfast/lunch/dinner
3 take the children to school
4 walk the dog
5 take the bus to school
6 make a sandwich
7 load the dishwasher

8 dust
9 mop the floor
10 wash the dishes
11 feed the baby
12 sweep the floor
13 vacuum the house
14 feed the dog
15 do homework

16 pick up the children
17 do the laundry
18 study
19 iron the clothes
20 go shopping

Did you make dinner yesterday?
Yes, I did.

Did you do the laundry yesterday?
No, I didn't.

A: **Did you go shopping yesterday?**
B: ....

A: **Did you .... yesterday?**
B: Yes, I did./No, I didn't.

Discussion
1 Which of these activities do you do every day?
2 Which activities do you like/dislike?

1 application form
2 résumé
3 cover letter
4 job interview
5 job candidate
6 interviewer
7 job announcement board
8 classifieds

① **Application For Employment**

PERSONAL INFORMATION

Name Cara Bridges
Address 325 Hillegrass Blvd.
 Berkeley, CA 94705
Telephone (510)123-45678 Social Security Number 164-41-8863
Job Applied for Senior accountant

WORK RECORD

Job title Asst. Accountant Company
Address 6318 Oak Street, San Fr.
 CA 94704 Telephone (5
How long were you at this job? 2 years

Job title Bank Teller Compa
Address See above
 Telephone
How long were you at this job? 1 year

READ AND SIGN

② Cara Bridges
325 Hillegrass Blvd.
Berkeley CA 94705
(510) 123-4567

Objective
A position as a senior accountant that uses my experience and produces an opportunity for growth.

Work Experience

4/00–present *Assistant Accountant* SUNCOAST BANK (San Francisco, CA)
 Worked in a busy office environment managing spreadsheets and accounts for national bank. Employee of the Month: August 2001.
10/98–4/00 *Bank Teller* SUNCOAST BANK (San Francisco, CA)
 Completed customer transactions in an efficient, friendly way. Maintained customer records and balances deposits.
1/98–8/98 *Server* PALM TREE CAFÉ (Santa Barbara, CA)
 Took customer orders and served food. Maintained high levels of cleanliness and customer satisfaction.
2/97–11/97 *Server* JOHNNY'S ICE CREAMS (Maryville, NY)
 Filled customer orders and ran a cash register. Washed dishes.

Education

6/97 BA ACCOUNTING Jamestown College (Jamestown, NY).

Skills and Experience

• Excellent Typing – 50 wpm
• Mac and PC use; competent with Work, Excel, and Powerpoint
• Fluent in Spanish
• California Bankers Association conference representative (2001–2002)

③
Cara Bridges
325 Hillegrass Blvd.
Berkeley CA 94705
(510) 123-4567

October 16, 2002

Ms. A. Helena Sole
Assistant Manager
Happy Helper Foods
P.O. Box 46
Calgary, Alberta T2N 2W1

Dear Ms. Sole,

I am writing to apply for the job of senior accountant at Happy Helper F was advertised in the *Calgary Herald*. As you can see from my resume have enclosed, I have three years of experience as a bookkeeper and bank t these positions I learned the importance of careful record keeping, and I hav gained valuable experience working as a member of a team.

Sincerely,

Cara Bridges

Cara Bridges

Enclosure

④ ⑤ ⑥

⑦ Vacancies

HELP WANTED

...TING. Accounts Payable. ...Receivable. Bookkeeping ...s. Data Entry. Payroll. All ...mporary/permanent. No ...fee. financialstaff.com. ...615-5555. jsmith@finan- ...m. Call 888-777-777.

...TING/ADMINISTRATOR ...degree. Responsibilities ...nancial statements, bud- ...casting. Must be com- ...y. P.O.S. system knowl- ...lpful. Good salary, ...efits. Apply in person, ...uare, Irish Pub & Grill, ...enue, San Diego or fax ...8-444-1233.

...NG CLERKS needed ...y for year-end work. ...will go through mid- ...st have 2 years experi- ...payables and receiv- ...ould be famili...

⑧ hire positions. Call weekdays, 8am-5pm, 888-320-475.

ASSISTANT/PERSONAL. Able to wear many hats. Flexible, energetic, and eager to learn. Office, sales, domestic, personal trainer, possible travel, and more. 888-444-666. x 222.

AU PAIR COORDINATOR. Promote cultural exchange in your community. Support local host families and au pairs participating in live-in childcare/cultural exchange program. Responsibilities include: Market-ing/networking, screening/interviewing host families, monthly au pair meeting. Openings in San Diego, South County, Temecula and surrounding areas. Work at home, flexible hours, compensation per family plus incentive program. Call 888-222-222 or visit www.aupair.org

Cleaners. We also need office entry and order help. Full/part-time positions. Experience preferred but will train. Apply in person, 0929 Williams Court.

BANQUET servers. Experienced, on call, weekdays and weekends. Paid weekly. Flexible hours. Please call Staffing, 8am-5pm, 888-222-0444.

BIKE CAB DRIVER. independent contractors. Male, female, full/part time. Driver's license. Train Monday, Tuesday or Thursday, 12.15pm, 646 19th Street, 888-949-0220.

BILINGUAL INTERVIEWERS. Spanish and English. No sales. Start your career in the interesting world of marketing research, conducting nationwide telephone surveys and opinion polls! Paid training. Full/part time. PM shifts, 7 days...ends...

Discussion

1 What should you include in a résumé?
2 What information does a job application ask for?
3 Where can you look for a job?

1 farmer
2 baker
3 mechanic
4 electrician
5 painter
6 truck driver
7 gardener
8 florist
9 window cleaner

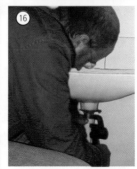

10 fisherman
11 sanitation worker/garbage collector
12 waiter/waitress/server
13 carpenter
14 chef/cook
15 butcher
16 plumber
17 grocery clerk
18 bagger
19 taxi driver/cab driver
20 bricklayer

DRIVING FOR AMERICAN'S FAMILIES
www.caregivercredit.org

What does she do?
She's a florist.

What does he do?
He's a waiter.

A: What does he/she do?
B: He's/She's a(n) ....

Discussion
1 Have you ever done any of these jobs?
2 Which of these jobs would you like to try?

1 veterinarian/vet
2 nurse
3 doctor
4 pharmacist
5 scientist
6 dentist
7 police officer
8 teacher
9 judge
10 lawyer
11 mail carrier
12 firefighter
13 professor, lecturer

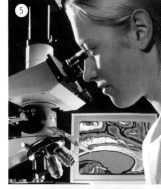

1 computer technician
2 architect
3 accountant
4 reporter/journalist
5 newscaster/anchor
6 receptionist
7 factory worker
8 travel agent
9 bank teller

10 real estate agent
11 telemarketer
12 photographer
13 model
14 hairdresser
15 artist
16 secretary
17 designer
18 salesperson

Would you like to be a photographer?
Yes, I would./No, I wouldn't.

A: **Would you like to be a newscaster?**
B: ....

A: **Would you like to be a(n)**
.... ?
B: Yes, I would./No, I wouldn't.

Discussion
Which of the jobs on the last three pages:
1 are very difficult?
2 are fun?

1 personal computer/PC
2 (desk) lamp
3 desk calendar
4 pencil holder
5 telephone
6 Rolodex
7 desk
8 in box
9 out box
10 tape/Scotch™ tape
11 white out™
12 eraser
13 (ballpoint) pen
14 hole puncher
15 stapler
16 rubber band
17 paper clip
18 notepad
19 wastepaper basket
20 datebook

21 pencil
22 filing cabinet
23 fax machine
24 photocopier

Do you ever use a PC?
Yes, I do.

Do you ever use paper clips?
No, I don't.

A: Do you ever use .... **?**
B: ....

Discussion
1 Which of these things do you have at school?
2 Which of these things do you have at home?

1 greet visitors
2 print a copy
3 work on a computer
4 answer the phone
5 conduct a meeting
6 participate in/attend a meeting
7 file papers

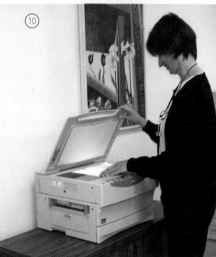

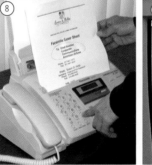

8 send a fax/fax a document
9 send an e-mail
10 photocopy a letter
11 staple documents together
12 fill in a form
13 sign a letter

What's she doing?
She's answering the phone.

What's he doing?
He's sending a fax.

A: **What's he doing?**
B: He's ....

A: **What's he/she doing?**
B: He's/She's ....

Discussion
1 Which of these activities are interesting?
2 Which of these activities are boring?

TOOLS

1 box cutter
2 toolbox
3 tape measure
4 saw
5 hammer
6 nail
7 power saw
8 plane
9 workbench
10 power/electric drill
11 (drill) bit
12 screwdriver
13 screw
14 hook
15 vise
16 sandpaper
17 pliers
18 wrench
19 ax/axe
20 paintbrush
21 (paint) can
22 (paint) tray
23 (paint) rollerpaint
24 paint

What's this?
It's a power drill.

What are these?
They're hooks.

A: What's this?/ What are these?
B: It's a(n)/They're
....

Discussion
1 Which of these things do you use?
2 Which of these things do you need?

1. time clock
2. time cards
3. machine
4. warehouse
5. loading dock
6. freight elevator
7. conveyor belt
8. safety glasses/
   safety goggles

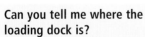

9. fire extinguisher
10. first-aid kit
11. pallet
12. forklift
13. foreman
14. worker
15. work station
16. dolly

Can you tell me where the loading dock is?
Sure. It's right over there.

Can you tell me where the goggles are?
Sure. They're right over there.

A: **Can you tell me where the**
.... **is/are?**
B: Sure. .... right over there.

Discussion

1 Which of these things do you have at your job?
2 Which of these things are necessary for safety?

1 construction site
2 crane
3 scaffolding
4 ladder
5 construction worker
6 hard hat
7 walkie-talkie
8 wheelbarrow
9 tool belt
10 girder
11 hook
12 excavation site
13 dump truck
14 ear protectors
15 jackhammer

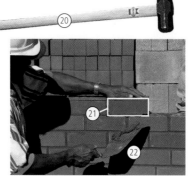

16 cement mixer
17 cement
18 backhoe
19 front-end loader
20 sledge hammer
21 brick
22 trowel
23 level
24 pickaxe
25 shovel

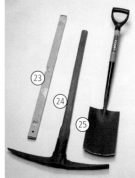

Have you ever used a pickaxe?
Yes, I have.

Have you ever used ear protectors?
No, I haven't.

A: **Have you ever used a(n)**
.... ?
B: Yes, I have./No, I haven't.

Discussion
1 Which of these things do people drive?
2 Which of these things make a lot of noise?
3 Which of these things could a person carry?

1 hotel
2 checking in
3 front desk
4 checking out
5 receptionist/desk clerk
6 guest
7 bellhop
8 suitcase
9 restaurant
10 conference room
11 elevator
12 maid/housekeeper
13 bar
14 lobby/foyer
15 bathroom
16 room key
17 single (room)
18 double (room)
19 room service

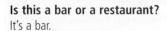

Is this a bar or a restaurant?
It's a bar.

Is she a receptionist or a housekeeper?
She's a housekeeper.

A: **Is this a(n) .... or a(n) .... ?**
B: It's a(n) ....

A: **Is he/she a(n) .... or a(n) .... ?**
B: He's/she's a(n) ....

Discussion
What is the difference between:

1 checking in and checking out?
2 a single room and a double room?

1 suspect
2 police officer
3 handcuffs
4 jail/prison
5 prison officer
6 inmate
7 courtroom
8 prosecuting attorney/prosecutor
9 jury
10 defense attorney
11 court reporter
12 witness
13 judge
14 evidence
15 bailiff
16 defendant

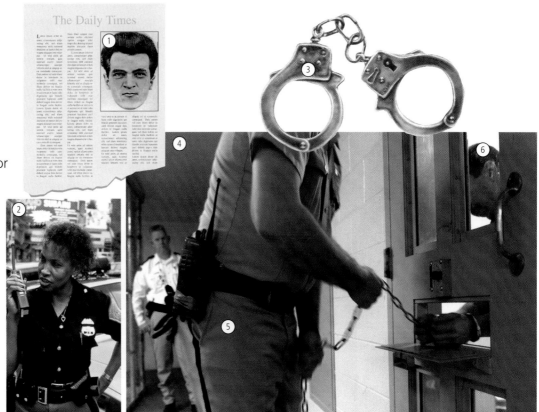

Is this the prosecuting attorney or the defense attorney?
It's the defense attorney.

Is this the witness or the defendant?
It's the witness.

A: Is this the lawyer or the court reporter?
B: It's the ....

A: Is this the .... or the .... ?
B: It's the ....

Discussion

1 Have you ever been a witness to a crime?

2 Do you watch any crime series on TV?

1 head
2 arm
3 back
4 waist
5 buttocks/ backside
6 leg
7 face
8 chest
9 stomach
10 hip
11 hand
12 foot
13 eye
14 eyebrow
15 nose
16 mouth
17 chin
18 hair
19 ear
20 lips
21 neck

22 nail
23 thumb
24 finger
25 wrist

26 palm
27 shoulder
28 forearm
29 upper arm
30 elbow

31 knee
32 thigh
33 shin
34 calf
35 ankle
36 heel
37 toe

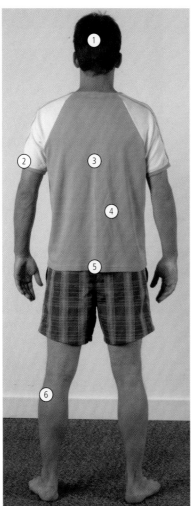
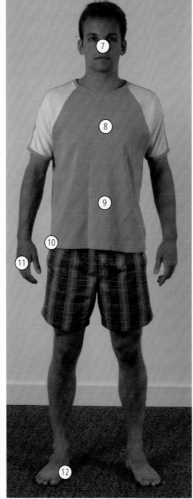
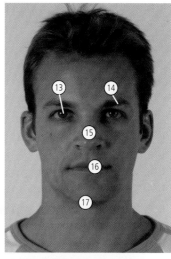
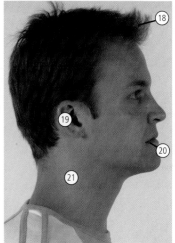

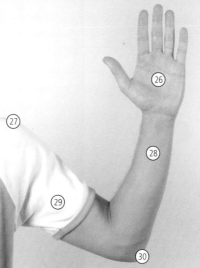
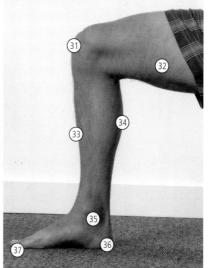

What's right above the eye?
The eyebrow.

What's right below the nose?
The mouth.

A: **What's right above/below the...?**
....

B: The ....

Discussion
What are the parts of the:
1 hand?
2 leg?

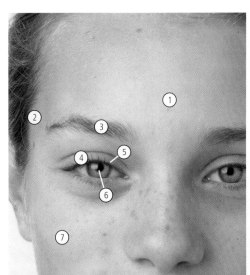

1 forehead
2 temple
3 eyebrow
4 eyelid
5 eyelash
6 pupil
7 cheek

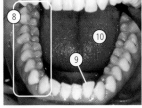

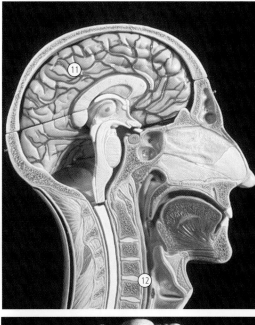

8 teeth
9 tooth
10 tongue

11 brain
12 throat
13 vein
14 artery
15 lung
16 liver
17 stomach
18 large intestine
19 small intestine
20 muscle
21 lung
22 heart

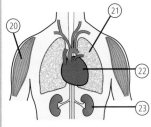

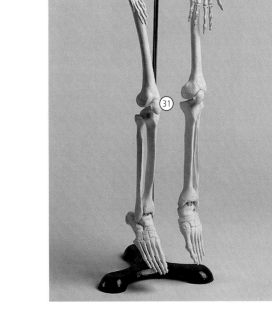

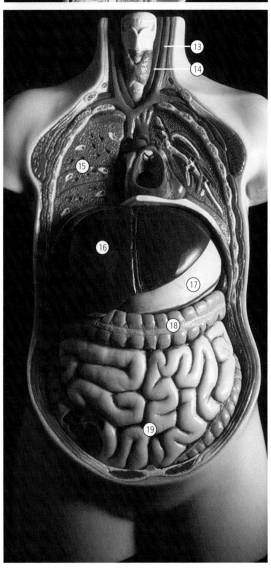

23 kidney
24 skeleton
25 skull
26 ribs
27 breastbone/
   sternum
28 spine/backbone
29 hip-bone
30 pelvis
31 kneecap

1 blond/light hair
2 red hair
3 brown/dark hair
4 black hair

5 long hair
6 shoulder-length hair
7 short hair

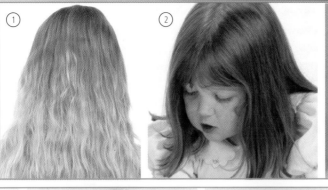

8 part
9 bangs

10 braid
11 pony tail

12 curly hair
13 straight hair
14 wavy hair

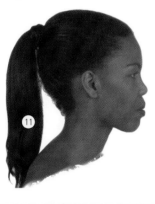

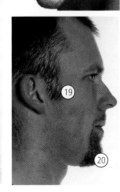

15 bald
16 stubble
17 mustache
18 beard
19 sideburns
20 goatee
21 short
22 tall
23 slim/thin
24 heavy

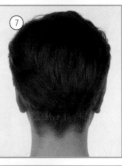

What does he look like?
He's thin, and he has short brown hair.

What does she look like?
She has curly, shoulder-length hair.

A: **What does she look like?**
B: She ....

A: **What does he look like?**
B: He ....

Discussion
1 What do you look like?
2 What do members of your family look like?

1 fall
2 talk/speak
3 carry
4 stand
5 touch
6 point
7 shake hands
8 sit
9 push
10 pull

11 laugh
12 hug
13 wave
14 lie down
15 cry

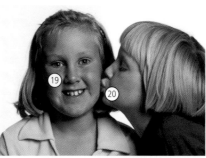
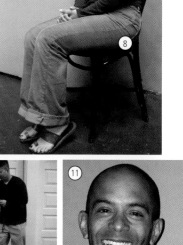

16 frown	19 smile
17 sing	20 kiss
18 clap	21 dance

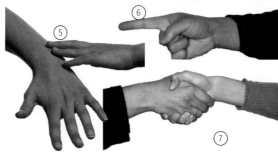

What's she doing?
She's waving.

What are they doing?
They're hugging.

A: What's he/she doing?/ What are they doing?
B: He's/She's/They're ....

Discussion
What do you do when you're:

1 happy?
2 sad?
3 tired?

1 read
2 pick up
3 put down
4 write
5 give
6 take

7 draw
8 cut
9 glue
10 press
11 tear
12 fold
13 paint
14 open

15 hold
16 fill
17 pour
18 stir
19 break

What's she doing?
She's reading.

What's she doing?
She's tearing paper.

A: What's she doing?
B: She's ....

Discussion
Take turns giving and following instructions.

1 wash/shampoo
2 shampoo
3 sink
4 rinse

5 hairdresser
6 towel dry
7 cape
8 cut

9   blow-dry
10 mirror
11 perm
12 style
13 highlights
14 roller/curler

15 comb
16 (hair)brush
17 styling brush
18 hairdryer
19 scissors
20 hand mirror

21 hairdresser's chair
22 footrest

23 massage
24 beautician
25 facial
26 towel

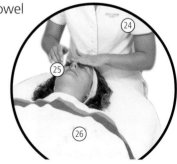

What's shampoo used for?
It's used for washing hair.

What are scissors used for?
They're used for cutting hair.

A: **What are curlers used for?**
B: They're used for ....

A: **What's (a/an) .... used for?**
B: It's/They're used for............................ .

Discussion
1 What does the hairdresser usually do to your hair?
2 Which of these things do you have at home?

A COSMETICS/MAKE-UP

1 moisturizer
2 blush/rouge
3 brush
4 foundation/base
5 eye shadow
6 mascara
7 lipstick
8 eyeliner
9 eyebrow pencil

B MANICURE ITEMS

10 nail clippers
11 nail scissors
12 nail file
13 emery board
14 nail polish

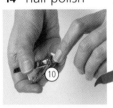

C TOILETRIES

15 perfume
16 cologne
17 shaving cream
18 aftershave
19 razor
20 razor blade
21 electric shaver
22 tweezers
23 brush
24 comb
25 hairdryer

Gel
Sensitive Skin

How often do you use mascara?
I sometimes use mascara./I never use mascara.

How often do you use an emery board?
I often use an emery board.

A: How often do you use (a/an)
.... ?
B: I never/rarely/sometimes/often/always
use (a/an) ....

Discussion

1 Which of these things are commonly used only by women? only by men? by both men and women?

2 Which of these things usually smell nice?

1 She has a **toothache**.

2 She has a **stomachache**.
3 antacid
4 Alka Seltzer™

5 He has a **headache**.
6 painkiller/pain reliever
7 aspirin
8 pills/tablets

9 He has **a cold**.
10 cold medicine
11 tissues

12 He has a **sore throat**.
13 throat lozenges

14 He has a **cough**.
15 cough syrup

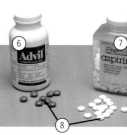

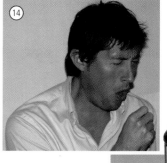

16 She has a **temperature/fever**.
17 thermometer

18 She has a **nosebleed**.
19 He has a **backache**.
20 He has a **broken leg**.

What's the matter with her?
She has a fever.
What's wrong with him?
He has a broken leg.

A: **What's the matter/ What's wrong with him/her?**
B: He/she has ....

Discussion
1 What do you take for a stomachache? a cold? a sore throat? a cough?
2 When is the last time you were sick? What was the matter?

21 She **fell down**.

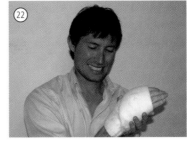

22 He **hurt his hand**.

23 He **sprained his ankle**.

24 bruise
25 sunburn
26 cut
27 scratch
28 bump

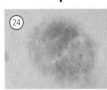

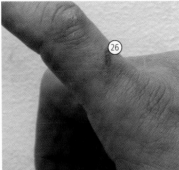

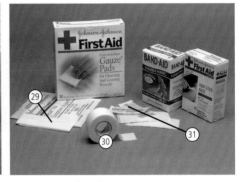

29 gauze (pad)
30 adhesive tape
31 adhesive bandage/Band-Aid™

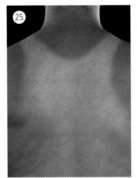

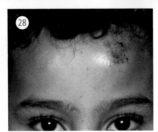

32 blood
33 black eye
34 scar

35 **insect/bug bite**
36 insect repellent
37 cream

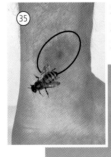

38 rash

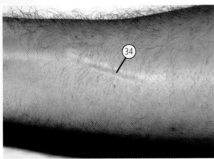

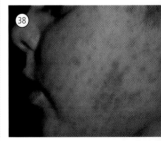

What happened to her?
She fell down.

What happened to him?
He got a bump.

A: **What happened to him/her?**
B: He/She ....

Discussion

1 Which of these remedies do you have at home?

2 What are some ways people can get a bruise? a sunburn? a cut? a bump?

THE DOCTOR'S OFFICE

1 height chart
2 patient
3 doctor/physician
4 examination table
5 X-ray
6 blood pressure gauge
7 scale
8 prescription
9 medical records
10 stethoscope

Feet
—7
—6
—5
—4

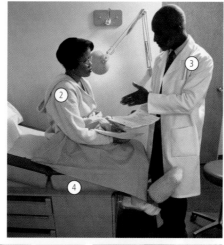

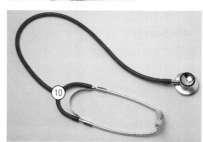

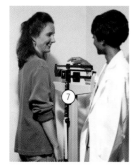

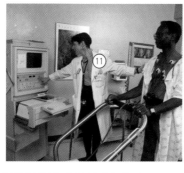

MEDICAL SPECIALISTS

11 cardiologist
12 ear, nose, and throat (ENT) specialist
13 pediatrician
14 obstetrician/gynecologist
15 ophthalmologist
16 osteopath
17 physiotherapist/physical therapist
18 counselor/therapist

What's this?
It's an x-ray.

Who's she?
She's a physical therapist.

A: **What's this** .... ?
B: It's a(n) ....

A: **Who's he/she** .... ?
B: He's/She's a(n) ....

Discussion

1 Do you always go to the doctor when you're sick?

2 Have you ever visited any of these specialists?

HOSPITAL WARD

1 doctor
2 nurse
3 patient
4 orderly
5 gurney
6 stitches
7 operation/surgery
8 mask
9 surgeon
10 surgical gloves
11 anesthetist
12 give a shot
13 syringe
14 needle
15 cast
16 wheelchair
17 crutches
18 waiting room
19 surgical collar
20 sling
21 scalpel

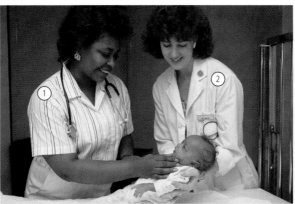

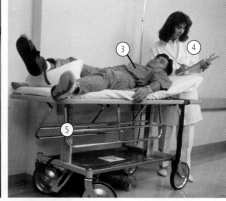

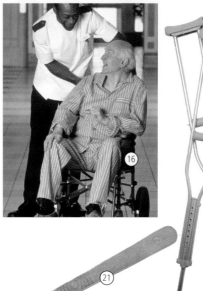

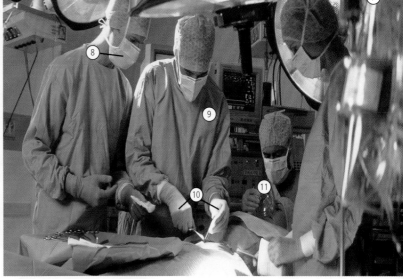

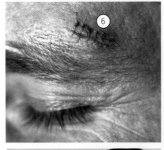

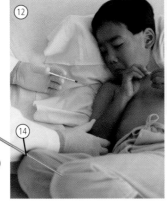

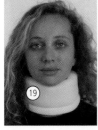

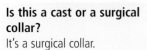

Is this a cast or a surgical collar?
It's a surgical collar.

Is she a nurse or an orderly?
She's an orderly.

A: **Is this a(n) ....
or a(n) ....** ?
B: It's a(n) ....

A: **Is she/he a(n) ....
or a(n) ....** ?
B: She's/He's a(n) ....

Discussion

1 Have you ever been in the hospital? Why were you there?

2 Do you like to visit people in the hospital?

DENTAL AND EYE CARE

A DENTAL CARE

1 dentist
2 drill
3 dental assistant
4 patient
5 (dental) hygienist
6 lamp
7 orthodontist
8 braces
9 dental floss
10 back teeth
11 front teeth
12 filling
13 gums
14 tooth
15 dentures
16 mirror

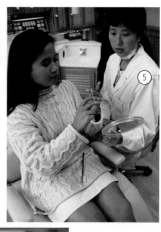
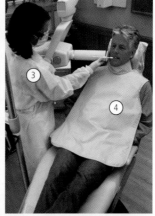

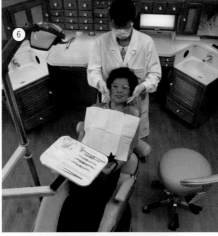

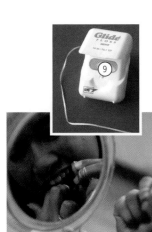

B EYE CARE

17 optometrist
18 eye chart
19 eyeglass case
20 glasses
21 lens
22 frames
23 contact lenses
24 eye drops
25 cleaning solution

Who's this?
It's the dentist.

What's this?/What are these?
It's a filling./They're glasses.

A: Who's/What's this?
B: It's the/a(n) ....

A: What are these?
B: They're ....

Discussion
1 Do you like to go to the dentist?
2 Do you wear eyeglasses/contact lenses?

OUTDOOR CLOTHING

1 rain hat
2 baseball cap
3 hat
4 umbrella
5 raincoat
6 jacket
7 coat
8 gloves

SWEATERS

9 turtleneck
10 V-neck sweater
11 cardigan
12 crewneck sweater

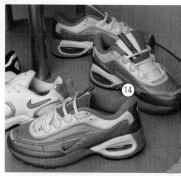

FOOTWEAR

13 shoes
14 running shoes
15 boots
16 sandals
17 pumps

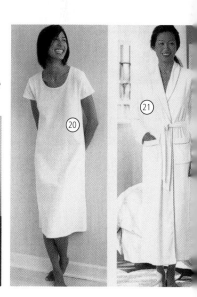

NIGHTCLOTHES

18 pajamas
19 slippers
20 nightgown/nightie
21 bathrobe

Do you prefer coats or jackets?
I prefer jackets.

Do you prefer sandals or boots?
I prefer sandals.

A: **Do you prefer** .... or
.... ?
B: I prefer ....

Discussion

1 Which of these things do you need in wet or cold weather?

2 Which of these things do you only wear at home?

CASUAL WEAR

1 pants/slacks
2 sweatshirt
3 T-shirt
4 shorts
5 jeans
6 blazer
7 overalls

UNDERWEAR

8 panties/underwear
9 ankle socks
10 slip/petticoat
11 panty hose/stockings/ nylons
12 tights
13 bra
14 socks

FORMAL WEAR

15 suit
16 jacket
17 blouse
18 skirt
19 dress
20 evening gown

What color is the T-shirt?
It's white.

What color are the tights?
They're black.

A: **What color is/are the**
.... ?
B: It's/They're (light/dark)
....

Discussion

1 Describe the clothes that you usually wear.

2 In your opinion, which type of clothes look best on a woman? on a man?

FORMAL WEAR
1 suit
2 tie
3 tuxedo
4 bow tie
5 vest
6 shirt

CASUAL WEAR
7 sweatshirt
8 jacket
9 shirt
10 pants/slacks
11 T-shirt
12 baseball cap
13 jeans

UNDERWEAR
14 undershirt
15 socks
16 boxer shorts/boxers
17 briefs/jockey shorts

SPORTSWEAR
18 warm-up suit
19 bathing suit/swimsuit
20 running shoes
21 bathing suit/swimming trunks

Do you like this vest?
Yes, I do.

Do you like these socks?
No, I don't.

A: Do you like this shirt?
B: ....

A: Do you like this/these
.... ?
B: Yes, I do./No, I don't.

Discussion
1 Describe the clothes that a classmate usually wears.
2 Which of these clothes are commonly used only at night? only during the day? both at night and during the day?

DESCRIBING CLOTHES

PARTS OF CLOTHES AND SHOES

1 collar
2 lapel
3 sleeve
4 buckle
5 shoelace
6 heel

7 buttonhole
8 button
9 hood
10 sole
11 hemline
12 pocket
13 seam
14 zipper
15 cuff
16 waistband

ADJECTIVES

17 short-sleeved
18 long-sleeved
19 wide
20 narrow
21 baggy
22 loose
23 tight

Do you like shoes with buckles?
Yes, I do./No, I don't.

Do you like baggy pants?
Yes, I do./No, I don't.

A: **Do you like** .... **with** .... ?
B: Yes, I do./No, I don't.

A: **Do you like** .... ?
B: ....

Discussion
Who in the class is wearing clothes and shoes with these parts?

COLORS

1 white
2 sky blue
3 yellow
4 navy blue
5 gold
6 pink
7 brown
8 dark green
9 purple
10 beige
11 cream
12 dark blue
13 red
14 gray
15 orange
16 black
17 turquoise

PATTERNS
18 striped
19 polka-dotted
20 patterned
21 solid
22 plaid
23 checked

What colors are in the checked pattern?
Navy blue and white.

A: What colors are in the
.... pattern?
B: ....

Discussion
1 Which of these clolors or patterns do you often wear?
2 Describe what the person next to you is wearing.

1 knitting needle
2 pattern
3 sewing basket
4 hook and eye
5 fastener/snap
6 thread
7 pincushion
8 thimble
9 needle
10 safety pin
11 pin
12 tape measure
13 scissors
14 yarn
15 Velcro™
16 iron-on tape
17 sewing machine
18 dressmaker/seamstress
19 tailor
20 stain

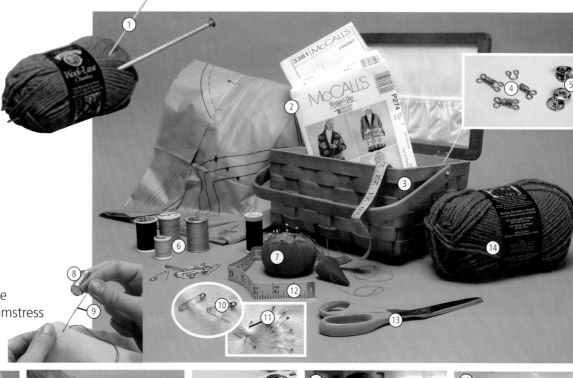

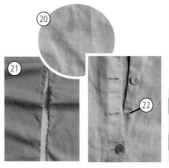

21 rip/tear
22 missing button
23 broken zipper
24 denim
25 wool
26 leather
27 linen
28 polyester
29 silk
30 cotton

Where's the sewing basket?
It's behind the pincushion.

Where are the scissors?
They're in front of the yarn.

A: Where's/Where are the
.... ?
B: It's/They're behind/in front of the
....

Discussion
1 Which of these things do you have at home?
2 What fabrics are you wearing today?

A JEWELRY

1 watch
2 chain
3 brooch/pin
4 necklace
5 earring
6 cuff link
7 tie clip
8 bracelet
9 barrette
10 pearls
11 ring

B METALS

12 gold
13 silver

C GEMS

14 diamond
15 emerald
16 ruby
17 amethyst
18 sapphire
19 topaz

D ACCESSORIES

20 daily planner
21 handkerchief
22 wallet
23 change purse
24 scarf
25 make-up bag
26 tote bag
27 clutch (bag)
28 purse/handbag
29 suspenders
30 briefcase
31 belt
32 buckle
33 key ring

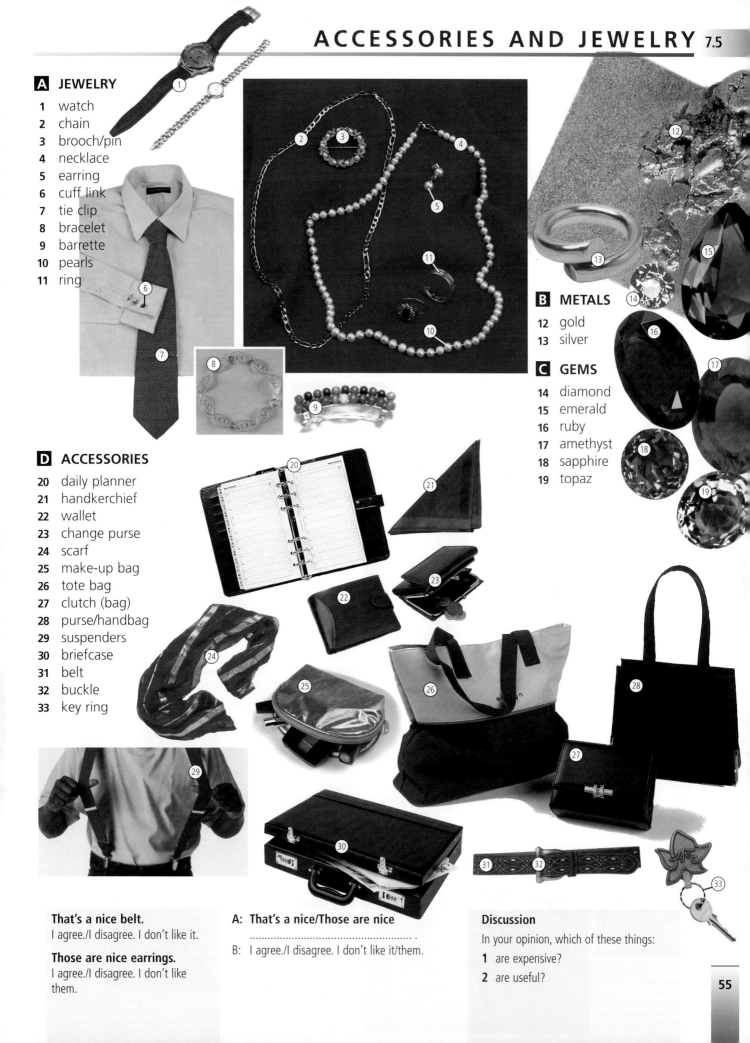

That's a nice belt.
I agree./I disagree. I don't like it.

Those are nice earrings.
I agree./I disagree. I don't like them.

A: **That's a nice/Those are nice**
....
B: I agree./I disagree. I don't like it/them.

Discussion
In your opinion, which of these things:
1 are expensive?
2 are useful?

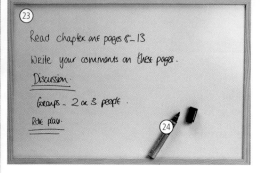

A SCHOOLS

1 nursery school/pre-school
2 kindergarten
3 elementary school
4 junior high/middle school
5 high school
6 college/university
7 graduates
8 technical/vocational school
9 adult education classes

B THE CLASSROOM

10 teacher
11 blackboard/chalkboard
12 desk
13 textbook
14 student
15 television
16 video cassette recorder
17 cassette/CD player
18 chalk
19 overhead projector
20 bulletin board
21 poster
22 computer
23 whiteboard
24 whiteboard marker

5 + 2 = 7

Read chapter one pages 8 - 13

Write your comments on these pages.

Discussion

Groups - 2 or 3 people.

Role play.

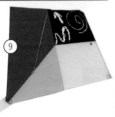

1 scooter
2 swings
3 jungle gym
4 bench
5 seesaw/teeter-totter
6 slide
7 sandbox
8 sand
9 kite
10 skateboard
11 tricycle
12 Rollerblades™
13 roller skates

14 easel
15 toys
16 doll
17 book
18 building blocks
19 coloring book
20 crayon
21 paints
22 paintbrush
23 safety scissors
24 jigsaw puzzle
25 glue

What color is the tricycle?
It's red.

What color are the building blocks?
They're yellow, blue, red, and green.

A: **What color is/are the**
.... ?
B: It's/They're ....

Discussion
1 Which of these things have wheels?
2 Which of these things did you have when you were a child?

8.3 THE SCHOOL

A CLASSROOM OBJECTS

1 triangle
2 ruler
3 protractor
4 compass
5 eraser
6 notebook
7 (ballpoint) pen
8 pencil
9 pencil sharpener
10 calculator

B THE SCIENCE LAB

11 tongs
12 bunsen burner
13 beaker
14 graduated cylinder
15 pipette
16 goggles
17 test tube

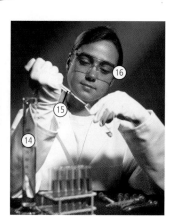

C THE GYM

18 mat

D THE COMPUTER LAB

19 screen
20 keyboard

E THE LANGUAGE LAB

21 headphones

F THE CAFETERIA

22 tray

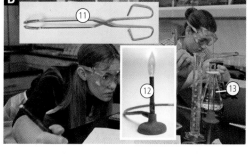
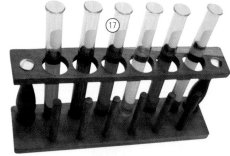

1 math
2 science
3 business studies
4 gym/P.E.
   (physical education)
5 social studies
6 art
7 languages
8 biology
9 chemistry
10 physics
11 shop/shop class
12 music
13 sociology
14 home economics
15 geometry
16 algebra
17 performing arts/drama
18 English literature

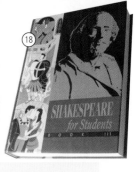

$2x + 35y = 54$

What are the students studying here?
They're in biology class.

A: **What are the students studying here?**
B: They're in .... class.

Discussion
1 Which of these subjects do/did you take?
2 What are/were your favorite subjects in school?

1 librarian
2 checkout desk
3 library card
4 reference section
5 books
6 shelf
7 terminal/computer
8 cart
9 periodicals section
10 magazines
11 newspapers
12 information desk

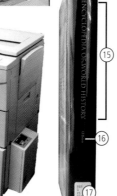

13 storytelling
14 photocopier
15 title
16 author
17 call number
18 dictionary
19 children's section
20 atlas
21 encyclopedia

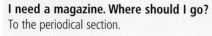

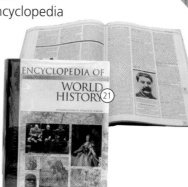

I need a magazine. Where should I go?
To the periodical section.

I need some information. Where should I go?
To the information desk.

A: I need a(n)/some ....
Where should I go?
B: To the ....

Discussion

1 How often do you go to the library?

2 What do you usually do at the library?

1 carrots
2 cabbage
3 cauliflower
4 onions
5 cucumbers
6 broccoli
7 brussel sprouts
8 leeks
9 pumpkin

10 zucchini
11 spinach
12 mushrooms
13 green onions
14 watercress

15 asparagus
16 lettuce
17 green beans
18 eggplant
19 peas
20 celery
21 corn (on the cob)
22 potatoes
23 tomatoes
24 garlic
25 green pepper
26 red pepper
27 artichoke

Should we buy cauliflower or broccoli?
Let's buy broccoli.

Should we buy green peppers or red peppers?
Let's buy green peppers.

A: **Should we buy** ....
 or .... ?
B: Let's buy ....

Discussion

1 Do you eat vegetables every day?
 Which do you eat most often?

2 Which of these vegetables can you eat
 without cooking them?

1 tangerine
2 grapefruit
3 lemon
4 lime
5 orange
6 grape
7 pineapple
8 banana
9 honeydew melon

10 avocado
11 kiwi
12 papaya
13 mango
14 apricot
15 starfruit
16 peach

21 apple
22 pear
23 watermelon
24 plum
25 strawberry
26 raspberry
27 blueberry
28 rhubarb
29 cherry

17 raisin
18 fig
19 prune
20 date

NUTS

30 hazelnut
31 walnut
32 coconut
33 Brazil nut
34 almond
35 peanut
36 cashew

Do you prefer apples or pears?
I prefer pears.

Do you prefer peaches or plums?
I don't like either.

A: **Do you prefer** .... or
.... ?
B: I prefer ..../
I don't like either.

Discussion

1 Which of these fruits are common in your country?

2 Which of these fruits do you like?

A CHECK-OUT AREA

1 aisle
2 groceries
3 check-out counter
4 customer/shopper
5 (check-out) cashier
6 conveyor belt
7 (shopping) cart
8 shopping bag

B FROZEN FOODS

C DAIRY PRODUCTS

9 eggs
10 yogurt
11 margarine
12 cheese
13 milk
14 butter

D JARS/CANNED FOOD

15 baked beans
16 tuna fish
17 soup
18 tomatoes
19 honey
20 corn
21 peanut butter
22 jelly

AT THE SUPERMARKET 2

DRY GOODS

1. coffee
2. tea
3. cocoa
4. cereal
5. rice
6. pasta
7. oatmeal
8. flour
9. cookies
10. sugar

CONDIMENTS

11. spices/herbs
12. salt
13. pepper
14. oil
15. vinegar
16. salad dressing
17. ketchup/catsup
18. mustard
19. mayonnaise

DRINKS

20. red wine
21. white wine
22. beer
23. mineral water
24. soft drink/soda
25. juice

HOUSEHOLD PRODUCTS

26. trash bags/garbage bags
27. plastic wrap
28. aluminum foil
29. window cleaner

What do we need today?
We need some coffee and some sugar, but we don't need any cookies.

A: What do we need today?
B: We need some ...., but we don't need any ....

Discussion
What would you buy to make:
1. breakfast?
2. a quick dinner?

A MEAT

BEEF

1 pot roast
2 steak
3 ground beef
4 liver

PORK

5 pork chops
6 sausage
7 bacon

LAMB

8 leg of lamb
9 lamb chops

CHICKEN

10 chicken

B DELICATESSEN/DELI

11 dip
12 coleslaw
13 potato salad
14 ham
15 salami
16 lunchmeat
17 Swiss cheese
18 American cheese
19 cheddar cheese

C FISH AND SEAFOOD

20 whole trout
21 scallops
22 oyster
23 lobster
24 crab
25 shrimp
26 mussels
27 fish fillet
28 salmon steaks

D BAKERY

29 whole wheat bread
30 bagels
31 pita bread
32 French bread
33 cupcakes
34 white bread

1 waiter
2 menu
3 wine list
4 dessert cart

APPETIZERS/HORS D'OEUVRES

5 shrimp cocktail
6 salad
7 soup

MAIN COURSES

8 roast beef
9 baked potato
10 stuffed peppers
11 pizza
12 lasagna

13 spaghetti
14 fish fillet
15 vegetables
16 rice
17 noodles

DRINKS

23 white wine
24 red wine
25 champagne
26 bottled water
27 coffee
28 tea
29 milk

DESSERTS

18 whipped cream
19 ice cream
20 cheesecake
21 pie
22 (chocolate) cake

I'd like the lasagna, please.
Certainly.

I'd like the cheesecake, please.
I'm sorry, we don't have any today.

A: **I'd like the .... ,
please.**
B: Certainly./I'm sorry, we don't have
any today.

Discussion
What would you like:
1 for dinner?
2 to drink?
3 for dessert?

1 milkshake
2 straw
3 soft drink/soda

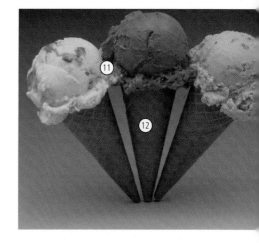

4 hamburger
5 hotdog
6 French fries
7 fried chicken
8 sandwich
9 taco
10 potato chips

11 ice cream
12 ice cream cone
13 doughnut/donut
14 muffin

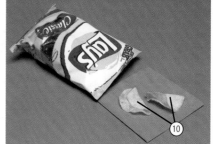

Would you like a hamburger?
Yes, please.

Would you like some doughnuts?
No, thanks.

A: **Would you like some potato chips?**
B: ....

A: **Would you like a(n)/some**
.... ?
B: Yes, please./ No, thanks.

Discussion
1 How often do you have fast food?
2 What's your favorite fast food restaurant? What do you usually order there?

CONTAINERS AND QUANTITIES

1 bag
2 can
3 jar
4 bottle
5 carton
6 loaf
7 tub/container
8 box
9 roll
10 tube
11 six-pack

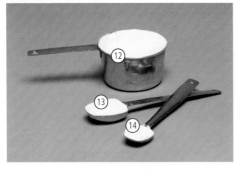

12 a cup
13 a tablespoon
14 a teaspoon
15 a gallon
16 a quart
17 a pint
18 a pound
19 an ounce

20 empty
21 a quarter full
22 a third full
23 half full
24 three quarters full
25 full

How much milk do we want?
Two quarts./ A gallon.

How many cans of soda do we want?
Three.

A: **How much** .... **do we want?/ How many** .... **of** .... **do we want?**
B: ....

Discussion

1 What do you usually buy in these containers (bags, cans, etc.)?

2 How much of these foods do you usually buy: milk, meat, bread, rice, fish?

1	wash
2	peel
3	grate
4	chop
5	crush
6	beat
7	cut
8	slice
9	grease
10	break
11	stir
12	mix
13	knead
14	steam
15	sauté
16	pour
17	weigh
18	boil
19	add
20	bake
21	stir-fry
22	grill
23	roast
24	barbecue
25	measure
26	fry

Is this crushing or chopping?
It's crushing.

Is this boiling or frying?
It's frying.

Is this .... **or**
.... **?**
B: It's ....

Discussion

1 In what different ways can you cook meat?

2 Explain how you make one of your favorite dishes.

1 grapefruit
2 hot cereal
3 milk
4 cereal
5 orange juice
6 butter
7 toast
8 croissant
9 coffee
10 tea
11 jam
12 bagel
13 cream cheese

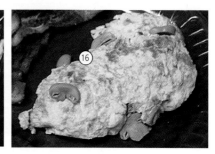

14 soft-boiled egg
15 scrambled eggs
16 omelet
17 fried egg
18 fried egg over easy

Would you like some scrambled eggs?
No, thanks. I'd rather have cereal.

Would you like some toast?
Yes, please.

A: **Would you like a(n)/some**
..........................?
B: No, thanks. I'd rather have a(n)/some
....................../Yes, please.

Discussion
1 What do you usually eat for breakfast?
2 Which of these foods would you like to try?

1 arrivals and departures board
2 train/railroad station
3 turnstile
4 passenger car
5 ticket
6 train
7 passenger

8 subway station
9 engine
10 track
11 timetable
12 escalator
13 platform

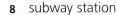

14 (taxi) driver/cab driver
15 taxi/cab
16 bus
17 luggage compartment
18 bus stop
19 bus driver

Do you want to go by bus?
No. Let's go by taxi.

Do you want to go by subway?
No. Let's go by bus.

A: **Do you want to go by train?**
B: No. Let's go by............................ .

A: **Do you want to go by .... ?**
B: No. Let's go by............................ .

Discussion

1 Which of these forms of transportation are used in your city?

2 Which of these forms of transportation do you use?

A CARS

1 hatchback
2 sedan
3 station wagon
4 four-wheel drive/SUV
5 convertible
6 sports car

B TWO-WHEELED VEHICLES

7 bicycle
8 wheel
9 pedal
10 motorcycle
11 motor scooter
12 moped

C OTHER VEHICLES

13 truck
14 van
15 trailer
16 minivan
17 motor home

E ENGINE

21 cylinder block
22 distributor
23 battery
24 air filter

D GAS STATION

18 gas pump
19 hose
20 nozzle

1 roof rack
2 windshield
3 hood
4 headlight
5 headrest
6 seat belt
7 door
8 gas cap
9 rear window
10 trunk
11 brake light
12 bumper
13 exhaust pipe
14 license plate
15 windshield wiper
16 side mirror
17 fender
18 hubcap
19 tire

20 clutch
21 brake
22 accelerator
23 rearview mirror
24 dashboard
25 steering wheel
26 turn signal
27 radio/cassette/CD player
28 gear shift
29 emergency brake

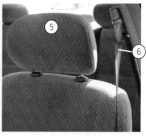

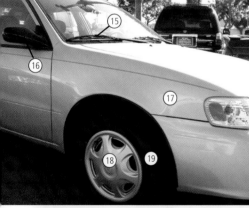

What's this – a van or a motor home?
It's a van.
What's this – the turn signal or the gear shift?
It's the gear shift.

A: **What's this – a(n)/the**
.... **or a(n)/the**
.... **?**
B: It's a(n)/the ....

Discussion
1 Do you have any of these vehicles?
2 Which are more common in your city: convertibles or station wagons? motorcycles or mopeds?

HIGHWAY

1 on-ramp
2 overpass
3 off-ramp/exit
4 street light
5 lane
6 shoulder
7 divider
8 reflector
9 toll booth
10 toll booth attendant

INTERSECTION

11 traffic light
12 red light
13 yellow light
14 green light
15 street
16 crosswalk

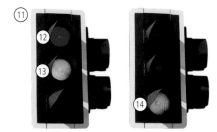

Is this a street light or a traffic light?
It's a street light.

Is this an on-ramp or an off-ramp?
It's an off-ramp.

A: Is this a(n) .... or
a(n) .... ?
B: It's a(n) ....

Questions for discussion

1 Do highways in your country look like this?

2 Do you have tollbooths in your country? How much is the toll?

1 bridge
2 railroad crossing
3 barrier

4 cone

5 one-way sign
6 stop sign
7 yield sign
8 railroad crossing sign
9 roadwork sign
10 slippery-when-wet sign
11 steep hill sign
12 no U-turn sign
13 no right turn sign
14 school crossing sign
15 do not enter sign
16 interstate highway sign
17 pedestrian crossing
18 speed limit sign

What does this sign mean?
It means "one way."

What does this sign mean?
It means "do not enter."

A: What does this sign mean?
B: It means " ...."

Discussion
1 Is there a bridge in your city? a train track?
2 What other road signs have you seen?

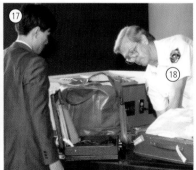

1 airline desk
2 ticket
3 boarding pass
4 immigration and naturalization

American Airlines
Flight AA 123   Name Mrs Smith
Depart 02 FEB   Dept. NEWARK
Gate 12 Seat 14a   Arrive NEW YORK
BOARDING PASS

5 passport
6 security checkpoint
7 metal detector
8 X-ray machine
9 carry-on bag
10 baggage/luggage
11 porter
12 baggage/luggage cart
13 suitcase
14 flight information

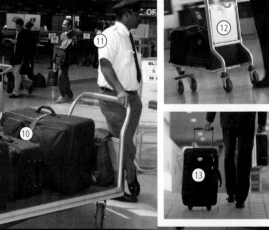

15 departure lounge
16 duty-free shop
17 customs
18 customs officer
19 baggage claim area
20 baggage/luggage carousel

21 cabin
22 window seat
23 middle seat
24 aisle seat
25 flight attendant
26 tray
27 window
28 armrest
29 cockpit
30 pilot/captain
31 instrument panel
32 copilot
33 oxygen mask
34 overhead compartment/bin
35 life jacket
36 takeoff
37 wing
38 runway
39 landing
40 airplane/jet
41 tail
42 air traffic controller
43 baggage cart
44 control tower
45 hangar
46 rotor blade
47 helicopter

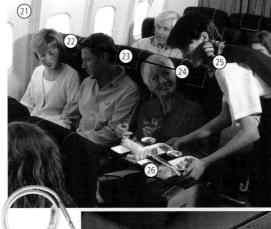

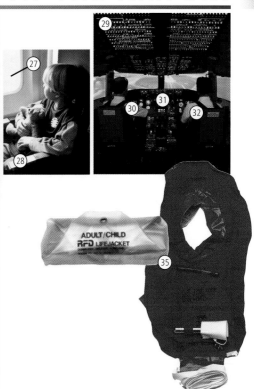

Where's the pilot?
He's in the cockpit.

Where's the plane?
It's on the runway.

A: **Where's the armrest?**
B: It's ....

A: **Where's the .... ?**
B: It's/He's/She's in/on the ....

Discussion

1 Would you like to work at an airport? What job(s) would you like to have?

2 Have you ever flown on a plane? Describe your flight.

1 Coast Guard boat
2 life jacket
3 cruise ship
4 oil tanker
5 ferry

6 sailing ship
7 anchor
8 cable

9 lighthouse
10 sailboat
11 marina
12 motorboat/ speedboat
13 cabin cruiser

14 rowboat
15 oar

16 cargo ship
17 crane
18 cargo
19 dock

20 yacht
21 deck

Have you ever been on a ferry?
Yes, I have.

Have you ever been on a yacht?
No, I haven't.

A: **Have you ever been on a**
.... ?
B: Yes, I have./No, I haven't.

Discussion
Which of these boats do you think is:
1 the slowest/fastest?
2 the heaviest?

1 bank
2 bank officer
3 ATM
4 credit card
5 ATM/debit card
6 bank teller
7 customer
8 cash drawer

9 traveler's check
10 foreign currency
11 checkbook
12 bank statement
13 withdrawal slip
14 (personal) check
15 stub

16 cash
17 dollar coin
18 fifty-cent piece/fifty cents
19 quarter/twenty-five cents
20 dime/ten cents
21 nickel/five cents
22 penny/one cent
23 one/one dollar (bill)/one dollar
24 five (dollar bill)/five dollars
25 ten (dollar bill)/ten dollars
26 twenty (dollar bill)/twenty dollars
27 fifty (dollar bill)/fifty dollars
28 one hundred (dollar bill)/one hundred dollars

Do you have change for a dollar?
Sure. Here are four quarters.

Do you have change for a twenty?
Sure. Here are two fives and a ten.

A: **Do you have change for a five-dollar bill?**
B: Sure. Here are ....

A: **Do you have change for a .... ?**
B: Sure. Here are ....

Questions for discussion
1 What kinds of bills and coins are there in your country?
2 How often do you go to the bank? use an ATM?

1	walk sign	**13**	parking meter
2	don't walk sign	**14**	traffic
3	pedestrian	**15**	traffic light
4	bus	**16**	street
5	crosswalk	**17**	bus lane
6	no parking sign	**18**	gutter
7	security camera	**19**	curb
8	department store	**20**	sidewalk
9	double yellow line	**21**	handrail
10	bus stop		
11	bus shelter		
12	road sign		

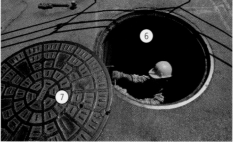

1 billboard

2 skyscraper
3 high-rise building

4 skyline
5 sky

6 manhole
7 manhole cover

8 bridge

9 fire hydrant

10 trash/garbage can

11 subway entrance

12 store/shop

13 vendor
14 magazine stand

Are there trash cans on the sidewalks in your city?
Yes, there are./No, there aren't.

Are there bus lanes on the streets in your city?
Yes, there are./No, there aren't.

A: **Are there .... on the sidewalks/on the streets in your city?**

B: Yes, there are./No, there aren't.

Discussion

1 Which of these things do you see every day?

2 Which of these things do you wish your city had?

1 mailbox

2 book of stamps
3 envelope
4 postmark
5 airmail letter
6 letter
7 postcard
8 address
9 zip code
10 stamp
11 (birthday) card

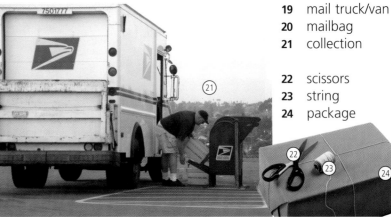

12 scale/meter
13 counter
14 postal clerk
15 customer

16 delivery
17 mail/letter carrier

18 mail
19 mail truck/van
20 mailbag
21 collection

22 scissors
23 string
24 package

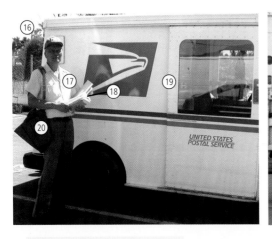

What's that?
It's a mailbox.

What are those?
They're stamps.

A: **What's that?/ What are those?**
B: It's a(n) ..../
They're ....

Discussion
How would you send these things:
1 a check to someone in another country?
2 a birthday present?

STATIONERY

1 white out™
2 Scotch™ tape
3 thumbtacks
4 pencil
5 eraser \
6 string
7 ballpoint pen
8 colored pen
9 (pad of) paper
10 (pack of) envelopes
11 glue stick

PERIODICALS, BOOKS, ETC.

12 ribbon
13 bow
14 matches
15 wrapping paper
16 (roll of) film
17 street map
18 newspaper
19 coloring book
20 paperback/book
21 magazine

CONFECTIONERY

22 (box of) chocolates
23 (bag of) candy
24 (bar of) chocolate/candy bar
25 (bag of) potato chips
26 (stick of) chewing gum
27 mints
28 lollipops
29 fudge

Can I have one of those maps, please?
Here you are.

Can I have some of that fudge, please?
Here you are.

A: **Can I have one of those/some of that ...., please?**
B: Here you are.

Discussion

1 Where do you usually buy these things?
2 What magazines do you like to read?
3 What kind of candy do you like?

1 music store
2 video store
3 pharmacy/drugstore
4 optician's
5 sporting goods
   store
6 candy store
7 toy store

8 mall
9 bookstore
10 card store
11 escalator
12 shoe store
13 fabric store
14 electronics store
15 clothing store

I need a TV.
Let's go to the electronics store.

I'd like some chocolate.
Let's go to the candy store.

A: **I need some tennis balls.**
B: Let's go to the ....

A: **I need/I'd like a(n)/some**
   ....
B: Let's go to the ....

Discussion:
1 Do you like to shop?
2 Where do you usually shop for clothes? books? shoes? CDs?

1 police officer
2 police station
3 police car

4 fire station
5 fire extinguisher
6 fire hydrant
7 fire engine
8 hose
9 smoke
10 fire
11 ladder
12 firefighter

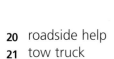

13 ambulance
14 accident
15 intravenous drip/IV
16 oxygen mask
17 stretcher
18 accident victim
19 paramedic

20 roadside help
21 tow truck

22 calling card
23 emergency number
24 pay phone
25 coin slot
26 receiver
27 number pad

$10

EMERGENCY - CALL 9-1-1

Have you ever been in an accident?
Yes, I have. I was in an accident last year.

Have you ever been in a tow truck?
No, I haven't.

A: **Have you ever been in a(n) .... ?**
B: Yes, I have. I was in a(n) ..../No, I haven't.

Discussion
1 What should you do in an emergency?
2 Would you like to be a police officer? a firefighter? a paramedic?

85

A FOOTBALL

1 football field
2 goalpost
3 goal line
4 yard line

5 guard
6 football
7 helmet
8 shoulder pads
9 referee
10 tackle

B BASEBALL

11 bat
12 batter
13 crowd/spectators
14 mask
15 home plate
16 catcher
17 pitcher
18 (baseball) glove/mitt
19 pitcher's mound
20 base
21 umpire
22 stadium
23 outfield
24 infield

A BASKETBALL

1 backboard
2 basket/hoop
3 net
4 basketball
5 (basketball) court
6 (basketball) player

B VOLLEYBALL

7 volleyball
8 net
9 (volleyball) player

C BOXING

10 boxing glove
11 boxer
12 boxing trunks
13 referee
14 ropes
15 boxing ring

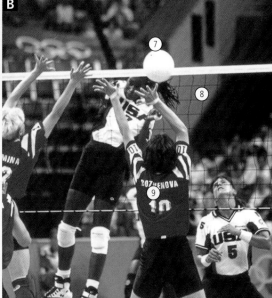

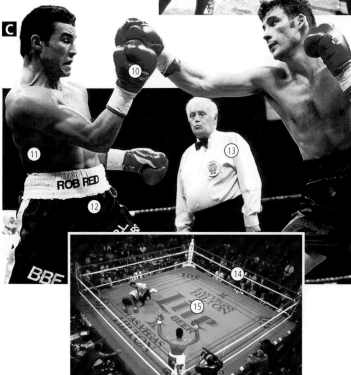

D HORSE RACING

16 gate
17 racehorse
18 jockey

Do they play football in your country?
Yes, they do./No, they don't.

Is boxing popular in your country?
Yes, it is./No, it isn't.

A: Do they play .... in your country?
B: Yes, they do./No, they don't.

A: Is .... popular in your country?
B: Yes, it is./No, it isn't.

Discussion
1 Do you play any of these sports?
2 Do you watch any of these sports on television?

INDIVIDUAL SPORTS 1

A TENNIS

1 (tennis) racket
2 (tennis) ball
3 (tennis) player
4 baseline
5 court
6 net

B BADMINTON

7 (badminton) racket
8 (badminton) player
9 birdie/shuttlecock

C PING PONG/TABLE TENNIS

10 (ping pong) ball
11 paddle
12 (ping pong) player
13 net
14 (ping pong) table

D MARTIAL ARTS

15 karate
16 blackbelt
17 judo

E BOWLING

18 pin
19 bowler
20 (bowling) ball
21 gutter
22 lane

F WRESTLING

23 wrestler
24 mat

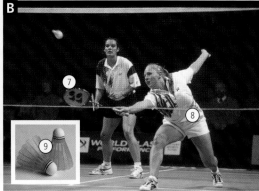

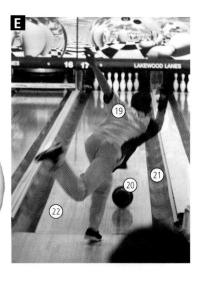

Would you like to try badminton?
Yes, I would./No, I wouldn't.

Would you like to try karate?
I've already tried it.

A: Would you like to try
....?
B: Yes, I would./ No, I wouldn't./ I've already tried it.

Discussion

Who are some famous:

1 tennis players?
2 wrestlers?
3 runners?
4 cyclists?
5 golfers?
6 gymnasts?

A **RUNNING**

1 runner
2 jogger

B **CYCLING**

3 helmet
4 cyclist
5 bicycle/bike

C **HORSEBACK RIDING**

6 rider
7 horse
8 saddle
9 stirrup
10 reins

D **GOLF**

11 golfer
12 (golf) club
13 (golf) ball
14 tee
15 hole
16 green

E **ROLLERBLADING**

17 helmet
18 rollerblader
19 elbow pads
20 in-line skate/Rollerblades™

F **GYMNASTICS**

21 gymnast
22 balance beam

G **ROCK CLIMBING**

23 climber
24 harness
25 rope

Did you go cycling last weekend?
Yes, I did.

Did you do gymnastics last weekend?
No, I didn't.

A: **Did you go** ....
climbing/do gymnastics/play golf last weekend?
B: Yes, I did./No, I didn't.

Discussion

1 Which of these sports need special clothes?
2 Which of these sports look like fun?

WATER SPORTS

A SWIMMING

1 goggles
2 swimming/bathing cap
3 swimmer
4 swimming pool

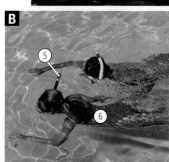

B SNORKELING

5 snorkel
6 snorkeler

C SCUBA DIVING

7 (air) tank
8 scuba diver
9 mask

D DIVING

10 diver
11 diving board

E SURFING AND WINDSURFING

12 surfer
13 surfboard
14 windsurfer
15 sailboard

H SAILING

22 sail
23 mast
24 sailboat

F ROWING

16 oar
17 boat
18 rower

G FISHING

19 fisherman
20 fishing rod
21 (fishing) line

I CANOEING

25 paddle
26 canoeist
27 canoe

J WATER-SKIING

28 water-skier
29 water ski
30 motorboat
31 towrope

A SLEDDING

1 sled
2 snow

B SKIING

3 downhill skiing
4 pole
5 (ski) boot
6 skier
7 ski
8 cross-country skiing
9 trail
10 snowboard
11 chair lift

C SKATING

12 figure skating
13 figure skater
14 ice skate
15 blade
16 speed skating
17 speed skater
18 ice

D BOBSLEDDING

19 helmet
20 bobsled
21 bobsledder

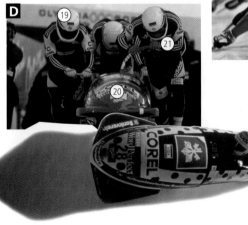

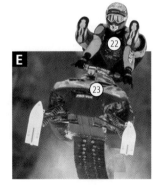

E SNOWMOBILING

22 snowmobiler
23 snowmobile

What are they doing.
They're downhill skiing.

What's she doing?
She's figure skating.

A: What's he/she doing?
B: He's/She's ....

A: What are they doing?
B: They're ....

Discussion

1 Which of these sports are popular in your country?

2 Do any famous skiers, figure skaters, or speed skaters come from your country?

1 rowing machine
2 (free) weights
3 mat
4 treadmill
5 exercise bike
6 aerobics class

ACTIONS

7 walk
8 kick
9 bounce
10 throw
11 catch
12 run
13 reach
14 hop
15 lift
16 kneel

17 bend over
18 stretch
19 do sit-ups
20 do push-ups
21 jump
22 jump rope

What's she doing?
She's stretching.

What are they doing?
They're running on the treadmill.

A: What's he/she doing?
B: He's/She's ....

A: What's are they doing?
B: They're ....

Discussion
1 Do you ever use any of this exercise equipment?
2 Which of these actions do you do when you exercise?

1 concert
2 baton
3 conductor
4 (symphony) orchestra
5 audience

6 ballet
7 ballerina
8 ballet dancer
9 ballet shoes

10 opera
11 singer
12 orchestra pit

13 theater
14 spotlight
15 aisle
16 stage
17 actor
18 actress

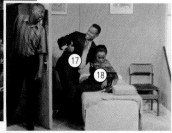

19 movie, film
20 (movie) screen
21 movie theater

22 band
23 drummer
24 singer/vocalist
25 guitarist

When did you last go to the theater?
I went two months ago.

When did you last go to the opera?
I've never been.

A: **When did you last go to a(n)/ the................ ?**
B: I went .... ago./ I've never been.

Discussion

1 What's your favorite form of entertainment? Why do you like it?

2 Who is your favorite entertainer? Why do you like him/her?

93

HOBBIES

1 coin collecting
2 coin
3 stamp
4 stamp collecting
5 magnifying glass
6 (stamp) album
7 baking
8 photography
9 camera
10 astronomy
11 telescope

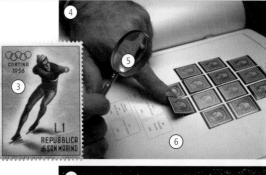

12 bird-watching
13 binoculars
14 gardening

ARTS AND CRAFTS

15 playing music
16 embroidery
17 quilting
18 sewing
19 knitting
20 knitting needle

21 sculpting
22 sculpture
23 painting
24 (paint) brushes
25 pottery
26 potter's wheel
27 woodworking

GAMES

1 video/computer games
2 chess
3 chessboard
4 chesspieces
5 checkers
6 checkerboard
7 dice
8 backgammon
9 cards

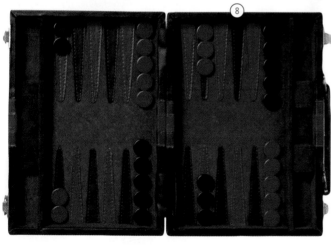

Do you like playing chess?
Yes, I do./No, I don't.

Do you like knitting?
I've never tried it.

A: **Do you like painting?**
B: Yes, I do./No, I don't./I've never tried it.

Discussion
1 What are your hobbies?
2 Which of these games can you play?

STRINGS

1 bow
2 violin
3 viola
4 (double) bass
5 cello
6 piano

BRASS

7 French horn
8 tuba
9 trumpet
10 trombone

WOODWINDS

11 flute
12 piccolo
13 oboe
14 recorder
15 clarinet
16 saxophone
17 bassoon

PERCUSSION

18 xylophone
19 drum set
20 cymbal
21 drum

ROCK MUSIC

24 mike/microphone
25 (electric) guitar
26 (bass) guitar
27 keyboard
28 amplifier

OTHER INSTRUMENTS

22 accordion
23 harmonica

Which is larger – a double bass or a cello?
A double bass is larger.

Which is smaller – an accordion or a harmonica.
A harmonica is smaller.

A: Which is larger/smaller – a(n)
.... or a(n)
.... ?
B: A(n) .... is ....
larger/smaller.

Discussion

1 Can you play any of these instruments?
2 Which instrument has the nicest sound?
3 Which instruments can be very loud?

1 (beach) umbrella
2 sandcastle
3 ocean/sea
4 pier
5 seashell
6 beach chair
7 sunglasses
8 shovel
9 bucket/pail
10 sand
11 sunbather
12 beach towel
13 lifeguard
14 promenade/boardwalk
15 beach ball
16 float
17 sunscreen/suntan lotion
18 bikini

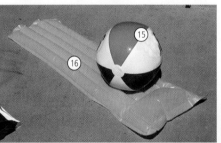

19 bathing suit/swimming trunks
20 bathing suit/swimsuit
21 cooler
22 wave
23 surfboard
24 surfer

What's this?
It's a beach ball.

What are these?
They're sunglasses.

A: What's this?
B: It's a(n)/the ....

A: What are these?
B: They're ....

Discussion

1 Do you like to go to the beach? How often do you go?

2 Which of these things do you usually take to the beach with you?

A BALLOONING
1 hot-air balloon

B FISHING
2 lake
3 boat
4 fisherman/angler
5 fishing rod
6 fishhook

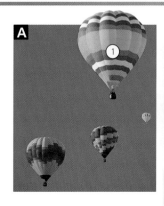

C HIKING
7 hiker
8 backpack
9 trail
10 signpost

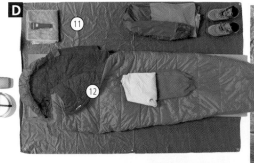

D CAMPING
11 ground cloth
12 sleeping bag
13 recreational vehicle/RV
14 campsite
15 tent
16 campfire
17 camper
18 picnic table
19 camping stove

Have you ever gone ballooning?
Yes, I have./No, I haven't.

A: **Have you ever gone**
.... ?
B: Yes, I have./No, I haven't.

Discussion
Which of these activities would you like to try?
Why?

1 botanical garden
2 roller coaster
3 Ferris wheel
4 amusement park
5 zoo

6 fairground
7 exhibition
8 museum
9 park
10 craft fair
11 tour guide
12 tourist
13 historic battlefield
14 national park
15 monument

Would you rather go to an exhibition or a craft fair?
I'd rather go to a craft fair.

Would you rather visit a museum or a park?
Neither. I'd rather visit a zoo.

A: Would you rather go to/visit a(n) .... or a(n) .... ?

B: I'd rather go to a(n) ..../Neither. I'd rather go to a(n) ....

Discussion

1 Which of these places looks the most fun?

2 Are any of these places near your home?

1 cat
2 whiskers
3 fur
4 basket
5 kitten
6 hutch
7 rabbit
8 cage
9 parakeet
10 hamster
11 (goldfish) bowl
12 goldfish
13 aquarium
14 tropical fish

15 gerbil
16 tail
17 guinea pig
18 doghouse
19 paws
20 dog
21 puppy

Do you have any pets?
No, I don't.

Do you have any pets?
Yes, I do. I have a dog and some goldfish.

A: **Do you have any pets?**
B: No, I don't./Yes, I do. I have (a/an)
....

Discussion
1 Which of these pets need a special "home?"
2 Which of these pets could you keep in an apartment?
3 Which of these pets needs to be outdoors?

1 donkey
2 (nanny) goat
3 kid
4 (billy) goat
5 turkey
6 bull
7 cow
8 calf
9 goose
10 gosling
11 duck
12 duckling
13 chicken
14 chick
15 rooster

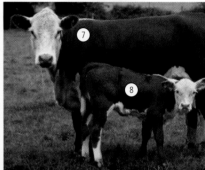

16 rabbit
17 sheep
18 lamb
19 ram

20 foal
21 horse
22 pig
23 piglet

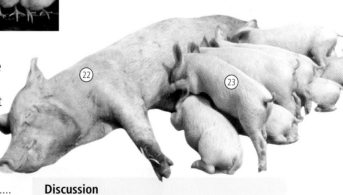

What's a baby pig called?
It's called a piglet.

What's a baby horse called?
It's called a foal.

A: **What's a baby .... called?**
B: It's called a(n) ....

Discussion

1 Which of these words refer only to male animals? only to female animals?

2 Which of these animals are on farms in your country?

1 elephant
2 tusk
3 trunk
4 lion
5 mane
6 tiger
7 bear
8 rhinoceros
9 horn
10 hippopotamus
11 kangaroo
12 pouch
13 cheetah
14 water buffalo
15 zebra
16 stripes
17 koala bear
18 giraffe
19 leopard
20 spots
21 deer
22 antlers
23 llama

24 gorilla
25 tortoise
26 polar bear
27 camel
28 hump
29 monkey
30 lizard
31 wolf
32 raccoon
33 alligator
34 crocodile
35 snake

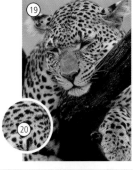

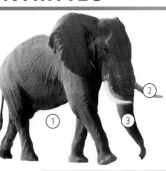

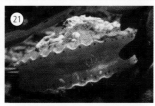

FISH

1 shark
2 tail
3 gills
4 fin
5 snout
6 bass
7 trout
8 scales
9 eel
10 angelfish

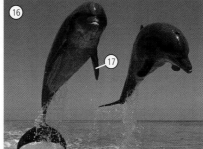

SEA ANIMALS

11 sea lion
12 killer whale/orca
13 shrimp
14 walrus
15 tusk
16 dolphin
17 flipper
18 crab
19 octopus
20 tentacle
21 clam
22 mussels
23 sea turtle
24 lobster
25 claw
26 starfish
27 jellyfish
28 seahorse

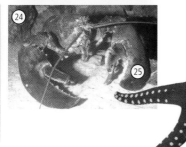

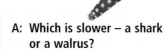

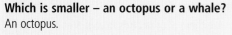

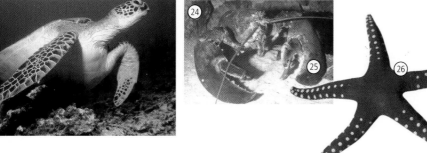

Which is smaller – an octopus or a whale?
An octopus.

Which is friendlier – a dolphin or a shark?
A dolphin.

A: **Which is slower – a shark or a walrus?**

B: ....

Questions for discussion

1 Which of these fish do people often eat?

2 Which of the sea animals can you sometimes find on land?

1 flamingo
2 pelican
3 crane
4 robin
5 penguin
6 flipper
7 cockatoo
8 crest
9 owl
10 swallow
11 ostrich
12 eagle
13 beak
14 falcon
15 stork
16 seagull
17 hummingbird
18 pigeon

19 nest
20 egg
21 bluejay

22 tail
23 peacock
24 feathers
25 parrot
26 swan
27 bill
28 wings
29 crow
30 claws

Are parrots prettier than pigeons?
Yes, they are.

Are hummingbirds bigger than robins?
No, they aren't. They're smaller.

A: Are .... prettier/ bigger than .... ?
B: Yes, they are./No, they aren't. They're ....

Discussion
1 Are there a lot of birds in your area?
2 Which of these birds do you see where you live?

INSECTS

1. wasp
2. beehive
3. bee
4. honeycomb
5. ladybug
6. mosquito
7. moth
8. butterfly
9. cockroach
10. dragonfly
11. caterpillar
12. snail
13. grasshopper
14. spider web
15. spider
16. ant
17. fly

SMALL ANIMALS

18. chipmunk
19. rat
20. skunk
21. mole
22. frog
23. mouse
24. groundhog/woodchuck
25. squirrel

Is this a moth?
Yes, it is.

Is this a squirrel?
No, it isn't. It's a chipmunk.

A: **Is this a(n)** .... ?
B: Yes, it is./No, it isn't. It's a(n)
....

Discussion

1 Which of these insects and animals are dangerous?

2 Which of these insects and animals can you sometimes find inside?

LANDSCAPE FEATURES

1 peak
2 mountain
3 lake
4 cactus
5 meadow
6 hill
7 valley
8 palm tree
9 desert
10 (sand) dune
11 reservoir
12 dam
13 pond
14 woods
15 pine cone
16 pine tree
17 forest
18 island
19 coastline
20 river
21 stream/brook
22 waterfall

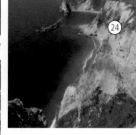
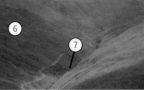

23 rock
24 cliff
25 beach
26 cave
27 grass
28 field
29 tree
30 swamp

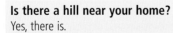

Is there a hill near your home?
Yes, there is.

Are there any fields near your home?
No, there aren't.

A: **Is there a(n)/Are there any**
.... **near**
......................................**?**
B: Yes, there is/are./No, there isn't/aren't.

Discussion
1 How many of these things are in your country?
2 What are the names of some famous mountains? lakes? islands? rivers?

SEASONS

1 summer
2 autumn/fall
3 winter
4 spring

WEATHER

5 rainy
6 sunny
7 snowy
8 icy
9 clear
10 cloudy
11 foggy

THERMOMETERS

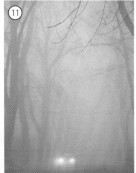

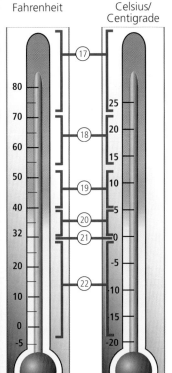

Fahrenheit   Celsius/
               Centigrade

80
70   25
60   20
50   15
40   10
32   5
20   0
10   -5
0   -10
-5   -15
         -20

17
18
19
20
21
22

12 hazy
13 windy
14 stormy
15 lightning
16 rainbow

TEMPERATURES

17 hot
18 warm
19 cool/chilly
20 cold
21 freezing
22 below freezing

What's the weather like?
It's foggy.

What's the weather like?
It's cloudy and cool.

A: What's the weather like?
B: It's .... and ....

A: What's the weather like?
B: It's ....

Discussion
1 What's your favorite season? Why?
2 What's your favorite kind of weather? Why?

1 Sun
2 solar system

A **THE PLANETS**

3 Mercury
4 Venus
5 Earth
6 Mars
7 Jupiter
8 Saturn
9 Uranus
10 Neptune
11 Pluto

12 orbit
13 star
14 constellation
15 comet
16 satellite
17 galaxy

B **THE MOON**

18 crescent moon
19 half moon
20 full moon
21 new moon

B

C **SPACE TRAVEL**

22 fuel tank
23 booster rocket
24 space shuttle
25 launch pad
26 astronaut
27 space suit
28 flag
29 lunar module
30 lunar vehicle

Where's Uranus?
It's between Saturn and Neptune.

Where's Mercury?
It's next to the Sun.

A: **Where's Jupiter?**
B: It's between .... and
   ....

A: **Where's Pluto?**
B: It's next to ....

Discussion

1 Do you know the names of any constellations?
2 Have you ever seen a comet?
3 Which planets have humans explored?

A HARDWARE

1 scanner
2 personal computer/PC
3 CD-ROM drive
4 floppy disk drive/A drive
5 hard drive/C drive
6 monitor
7 screen
8 keyboard
9 speaker
10 printer
11 mouse pad
12 mouse
13 floppy (disk)/diskette
14 laptop
15 CD-ROM

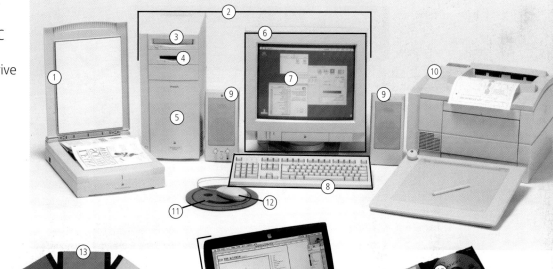

B SOFTWARE

16 spreadsheet
17 window
18 icon
19 document
20 toolbar
21 cursor

What's this called?
It's a laptop.

What's this called?
It's an icon.

A: What's this called?
B: It's a(n) ....

Discussion

1 Do you use a computer at home or work?
2 What can people do on a computer?

1 DVD player
2 DVD

3 video (cassette)
4 remote (control)
5 video cassette recorder/VCR

6 television/TV
7 TV screen

8 games console
9 video games

10 clock radio

11 stereo system/hi-fi
12 compact disc/CD player
13 compact disc/CD
14 tape deck/cassette deck
15 tape/cassette
16 radio
17 tuner
18 speaker
19 computer
20 personal cassette player/Walkman™
21 headphones

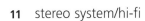

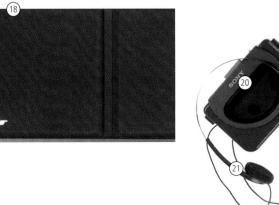

1 cell phone/cellular phone/mobile (phone)
2 charger
3 telephone/phone
4 answering machine
5 cordless phone
6 base
7 keypad
8 handset
9 adapter plug
10 (pocket) calculator
11 pager
12 electronic personal organizer/
PDA

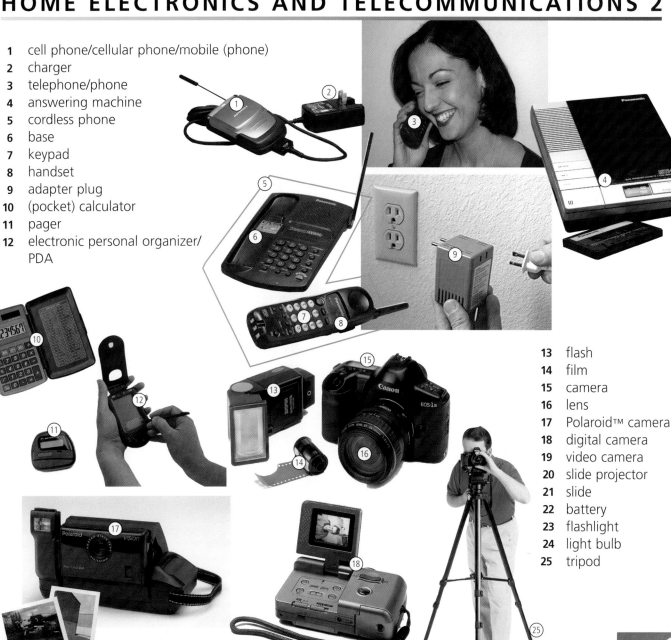

13 flash
14 film
15 camera
16 lens
17 Polaroid™ camera
18 digital camera
19 video camera
20 slide projector
21 slide
22 battery
23 flashlight
24 light bulb
25 tripod

Which is more useful – a Polaroid camera or a digital camera?
I think a digital camera is more useful.

Which is more useful – a VCR or a DVD player?
I think a VCR is more useful.

A: Which is more useful – a(n)
.... or a(n)
.... ?
B: I think a(n) ....
is more useful.

Discussion
1 Which of these things do you have?
2 Which of these things would you like to have?

FEELINGS

1 sad
2 nervous
3 confused
4 angry/mad
5 excited
6 surprised
7 bored
8 happy
9 scared/afraid
10 suspicious

Is she happy?
Yes, she is./No, she isn't. She's bored

Does he look confused?
Yes, he does./No, he doesn't. He looks
scared

A: Is he/she .... ?
B: Yes, he/she is./No, he/she isn't.

A: Does he/she look .... ?
B: Yes, he/she does./No, he/she doesn't.

Discussion

When do you feel:

1 nervous?
2 angry?
3 happy?

OPPOSITES

1 neat
2 messy

3 dry
4 wet

5 tight
6 loose

7 heavy
8 light

9 open
10 closed

11 short
12 long

13 empty
14 full

15 rough
16 smooth

17 near/close
18 far

19 light
20 dark

21 on
22 off

23 thin
24 thick

25 narrow
26 wide

27 deep
28 shallow

29 cheap
30 expensive

31 fast
32 slow

33 hard
34 soft

$5.00 $10,000

Is it wet or dry?
It's wet.

Is he far or near?
He's near.

A: Is it light or heavy?
B: It's ....

A: Is it/he .... or .... ?
B: It's/He's ....

Discussion

What are other things that can be decribed with these adjectives?

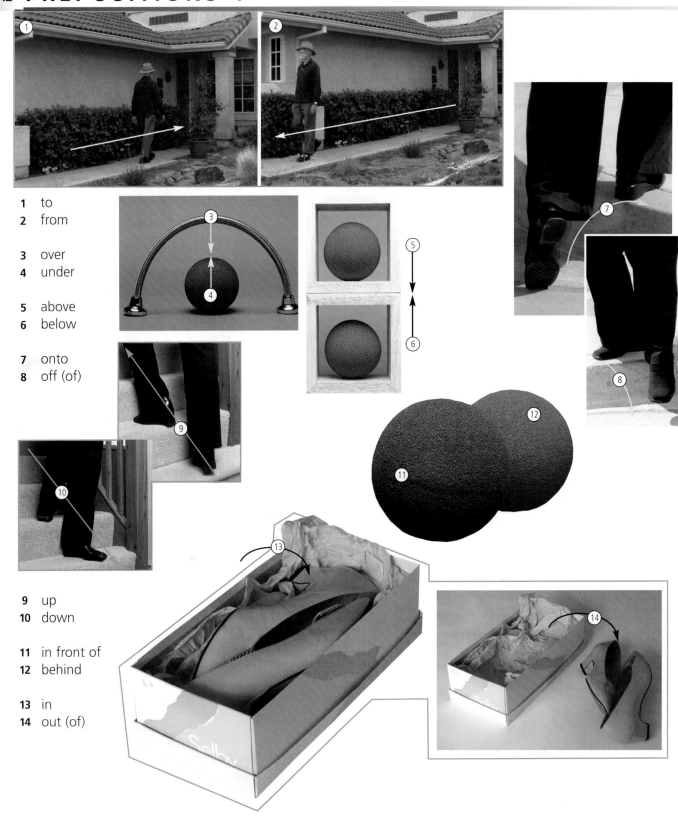

1	to
2	from
3	over
4	under
5	above
6	below
7	onto
8	off (of)
9	up
10	down
11	in front of
12	behind
13	in
14	out (of)

Does this picture show up or down?
It shows up.

Does this show in front of or behind?
Behind.

A: Does this show to or from?
B: It shows ....

Discussion
How many of these prepositions can you demonstrate?

1 around
2 between
3 against
4 across
5 away from
6 toward/towards
7 outside
8 inside
9 into
10 through
11 out of
12 along
13 beside/next to

14 at the top
15 in the middle
16 at the bottom

17 on top (of)
18 under/underneath

Where is this tire?
It's at the top.

Where is this ball?
It's outside the box.

A: **Where is this** .... ?
B: It's ....

Discussion

Who is sitting:

1 next to you?
2 across from you?
3 in the middle of the room?

beef /bif/ **65**

beehive /'bihaɪv/ **105**

beer /bɪr/ **64**

behind /bɪ'haɪnd/ **115**

beige /beɪʒ/ **53**

bellhop /'bɛlhɑp/ **35**

below /bɪ'loʊ/ **115**

below freezing /bɪ,loʊ 'frizɪŋ/ **107**

belt /bɛlt/ **55**

bench /bɛntʃ/ **57**

bend over /,bɛnd 'oʊvɚ/ **92**

beside /bɪ'saɪd/ **116**

between /bɪ'twin/ **116**

bib /bɪb/ **20**

bicycle /'baɪsɪkəl/ **72, 89**

bike /baɪk/ **89**

bikini /bɪ'kini/ **97**

bill /bɪl/ **104**

billboard /'bɪlbɔrd/ **81**

billy goat /'bɪli ,goʊt/ **101**

binoculars /bɪ'nɑkyəlɚz/ **94**

biology /baɪ'ɑlədʒi/ **59**

birds /bɚdz/ **104**

birdie /'bɚdi/ **88**

bird-watching /'bɚd ,wɑtʃɪŋ/ **94**

Birmingham /'bɚmɪŋ,hæm/ **8**

birthday card /'bɚθdeɪ ,kɑrd/ **82**

Bismarck /'bɪzmɑrk/ **8**

black eye /,blæk 'aɪ/ **45**

black hair /,blæk 'hɛr/ **39**

black /blæk/ **53**

blackbelt /'blækbɛlt/ **88**

blackboard /'blækbɔrd/ **56**

blade /bleɪd/ **91**

blazer /'bleɪzɚ/ **50**

blender /'blɛndɚ/ **15**

blond hair /,blɑnd 'hɛr/ **39**

blood /blʌd/ **45**

blood pressure gauge /'blʌd ,prɛʃɚ ,geɪdʒ/ **46**

blouse /blaʊs/ **50**

blow-dry /bloʊdraɪ/ **42**

blueberry /'blu,bɛri/ **62**

bluejay /'bludʒeɪ/ **104**

blush /blʌʃ/ **43**

boarding pass /'bɔrdɪŋ ,pæs/ **76**

boardwalk /'bɔrdwɔk/ **97**

boat /boʊt/ **90, 98**

bobsled /'bɑbslɛd/ **91**

bobsledder /'bɑbslɛdɚ/ **91**

bobsledding /'bɑb,slɛdɪŋ/ **91**

body /'bɑdi/ **37**

boil /bɔɪl/ **69**

Boise /'bɔɪzi/ **8**

book /bʊk/ **18, 57, 60, 83**

bookcase /'bʊk-keɪs/ **18**

book of stamps /,bʊk əv 'stæmps/ **82**

bookstore /'bʊkstɔr/ **84**

booster rocket /'bustɚ ,rɑkɪt/ **108**

boots /buts/ **49**

bored /bɔrd/ **113**

Boston /'bɔstən/ **8**

botanical garden /bə'tænɪkəl ,gɑrdn/ **99**

bottle /'bɑtl/ **68**

bottle opener /'bɑtl ,oʊpənɚ/ **15**

bottled water /,bɑtld 'wɔtɚ/ **66**

bounce /baʊns/ **92**

bow /boʊ/ **83, 96**

bow tie /'boʊ taɪ/ **51**

bowl /boʊl/ **19**

bowler /'boʊlɚ/ **88**

bowling /'boʊlɪŋ/ **88**

bowling ball /'boʊlɪŋ ,bɔl/ **88**

box /bɑks/ **68**

box cutter /'bɑks ,kʌtɚ/ **32**

boxer /'bɑksɚ/ **87**

boxer shorts /'bɑksɚ ,ʃɔrts/ **51**

boxers /bɑksɚz/ **51**

boxing /'bɑksɪŋ/ **87**

boxing glove /'bɑksɪŋ ,glʌv/ **87**

boxing ring /'bɑksɪŋ ,rɪŋ/ **87**

boxing trunks /'bɑksɪŋ ,trʌŋks/ **87**

box of tissues /,bɑks əv 'tɪʃuz/ **16**

boy /bɔɪ/ **9**

bra /brɑ/ **50**

bracelet /'breɪslɪt/ **55**

braces /'breɪsɪz/ **48**

braid /breɪd/ **39**

brain /breɪn/ **38**

brake /breɪk/ **73**

brake light /'breɪk laɪt/ **73**

brass /bræs/ **96**

brazil nut /brə'zɪl ,nʌt/ **62**

break /breɪk/ **41, 69**

breakfast /'brɛkfəst/ **70**

breastbone /'brɛstboʊn/ **38**

brick /brɪk/ **34**

bricklayer /'brɪk,leɪɚ/ **27**

bridge /brɪdʒ/ **75, 81**

briefcase /'brifkeɪs/ **55**

briefs /brifs/ **51**

broccoli /'brɑkəli/ **61**

broken leg /,broʊkən 'lɛg/ **44**

broken zipper /,broʊkən 'zɪpɚ/ **54**

brooch /broʊtʃ/ **55**

brook /brʊk/ **106**

broom /brum/ **21**

brother /'brʌðɚ/ **10**

brother-in-law /'brʌðɚ ɪn ,lɔ/ **11**

brown /braʊn/ **53**

brown hair /,braʊn 'hɛr/ **39**

bruise /bruz/ **45**

brush /brʌʃ/ **21, 43, 94**

brush your hair /,brʌʃ yɚ 'hɛr/ **12**

brush your teeth /,brʌʃ yɚ 'tiθ/ **12**

brussel sprouts /'brʌsəl ,spraʊts/ **61**

bucket /'bʌkɪt/ **21, 97**

buckle /'bʌkəl/ **52, 55**

Buffalo /'bʌfə,loʊ/ **8**

bug bite /'bʌg baɪt/ **45**

building blocks /'bɪldɪŋ ,blɑks/ **57**

bull /bʊl/ **101**

bulletin board /'bʊlətn ,bɔrd/ **56**

bump /bʌmp/ **45**

bumper /'bʌmpɚ/ **73**

bunsen burner /'bʌnsən ,bɚnɚ/ **58**

burner /'bɚnɚ/ **14**

bus /bʌs/ **71, 80**

bus driver /'bʌs ,draɪvɚ/ **71**

bush /bʊʃ/ **22**

business studies /'bɪznɪs ,stʌdiz/ **59**

bus lane /'bʌs leɪn/ **80**

bus shelter /'bʌs ,ʃɛltɚ/ **80**

bus stop /'bʌs stɑp/ **71, 80**

butcher /'bʊtʃɚ/ **27**

butter /'bʌtɚ/ **63, 70**

butterfly /'bʌtɚ,flaɪ/ **105**

buttocks /'bʌtəks/ **37**

button /'bʌtn/ **52**

buttonhole /'bʌtn,hoʊl/ **52**

cab /kæb/ **71**

cabbage /'kæbɪdʒ/ **61**

cabin /'kæbɪn/ **77**

cab driver /'kæb ,draɪvɚ/ **27**

cabin cruiser /'kæbɪn ,kruzɚ/ **78**

cabinet /'kæbənɪt/ **14**

cable /'keɪbəl/ **78**

cactus /'kæktəs/ **106**

cafeteria /,kæfə'tɪriə/ **58**

cage /keɪdʒ/ **100**

calculator /'kælkyə,leɪtɚ/ **58, 111**

calf /kæf/ **37, 101**

California /,kælɪ'fɔrnyə/ **8**

calling card /'kɔlɪŋ ,kɑrd/ **85**

call number /'kɔl ,nʌmbɚ/ **60**

camel /'kæməl/ **102**

camera /'kæmrə/ **94, 111**

camper /'kæmpɚ/ **98**

campfire /'kæmpfaɪɚ/ **98**

camping /'kæmpɪŋ/ **98**

camping stove /'kæmpɪŋ ,stoʊv/ **98**

campsite /'kæmpsaɪt/ **98**

can /kæn/ **68**

Canada /'kænədə/ **8**

candy /'kændi/ **83**

candy bar /'kændi ,bɑr/ **83**

candy store /'kændi ,stɔr/ **84**

canned food /,kænd 'fud/ **63**

canoe /kə'nu/ **90**

canoeing /kə'nuɪŋ/ **90**

canoeist /kə'nuɪst/ **90**

can opener /'kæn ,oʊpənɚ/ **15**

cape /keɪp/ **42**

captain /'kæptən/ **77**

car /kɑr/ **72, 98**

card store /'kɑrd stɔr/ **84**

cardigan /'kɑrdəgən/ **49**

cardiologist /,kɑrdi'ɑlədʒɪst/ **46**

cards /kɑrdz/ **95**

cargo ship /'kɑrgoʊ ,ʃɪp/ **78**

cargo /'kɑrgoʊ/ **78**

carpenter /'kɑrpəntɚ/ **27**

carpet /'kɑrpɪt/ **17**

carrots /'kærəts/ **61**

carry /'kæri/ **40**

carry-on bag /'kæri ɔn ,bæg/ **76**

car seat /'kɑr sit/ **20**

Carson City /,kɑrsən 'sɪti/ **8**

cart /kɑrt/ **60**

carton /'kɑrtn/ **68**

cash /kæʃ/ **79**

cash drawer /'kæʃ drɔr/ **79**

cashew /'kæʃu/ **62**

cashier /kæ'ʃɪr/ **63**

cassette /kə'sɛt/ **110**

cassette deck /kə'sɛt ,dɛk/ **110**

cassette player /kə'sɛt ,pleɪɚ/ **56, 73**

cast /kæst/ **47**

casual wear /'kæʒuəl ,wɛr/ **50, 51**

cat /kæt/ **100**

catch /kætʃ/ **92**

catcher /'kætʃɚ/ **86**

caterpillar /'kætɚ,pɪlɚ/ **105**

catsup /'kɛtʃəp/ **64**

cauliflower /'kɔlɪ,flaʊɚ/ **61**

cave /keɪv/ **106**

CD /,si 'di/ **110**

CD player /,si 'di ,pleɪɚ/ **56, 73, 110**

C drive /'si draɪv/ **109**

CD-ROM /,si di 'rɑm/ **109**

CD-ROM drive /,si di 'rɑm ,draɪv/ **109**

ceiling /'silɪŋ/ **24**

celery /'sɛləri/ **61**

cellar /'sɛlɚ/ **24**

cello /'tʃɛloʊ/ **96**

cell phone /'sɛl foʊn/ **111**

cellular phone /,sɛlyəlɚ 'foʊn/ **111**

cement /sɪ'mɛnt/ **34**

cement mixer /sɪ'mɛnt ,mɪksɚ/ **34**

center /'sɛntɚ/ **5**

cents /sɛnts/ **79**

cereal /'sɪriəl/ **64, 70**

chain /tʃeɪn/ **55**

chair /tʃɛr/ **19**

chair lift /'tʃɛr lɪft/ **91**

chalk /tʃɔk/ **56**

chalkboard /'tʃɔkbɔrd/ **56**

champagne /ʃæm'peɪn/ **66**

chandelier /ˌʃændə'lɪr/ **19**

change purse /'tʃeɪndʒ pɚs/ **55**

changing pad /'tʃeɪndʒɪŋ ˌpæd/ **20**

charger /'tʃɑrdʒɚ/ **111**

Charleston /'tʃɑrlstən/ **8**

Charlotte /'ʃɑrlət/ **8**

cheap /tʃip/ **114**

checkbook /'tʃɛkbʊk/ **79**

checked /tʃɛkt/ **53**

checkerboard /'tʃɛkɚbɔrd/ **95**

checkers /'tʃɛkɚz/ **95**

checking in /ˌtʃɛkɪŋ 'ɪn/ **35**

checking out /ˌtʃɛkɪŋ 'aʊt/ **35**

check-out area /'tʃɛkaʊt ˌɛriə/ **63**

check-out cashier /'tʃɛkaʊt kæˌʃɪr/ **63**

check-out counter /'tʃɛkaʊt ˌkaʊntɚ/ **63**

checkout desk /'tʃɛk-aʊt ˌdɛsk/ **60**

cheddar cheese /ˌtʃɛdɚ 'tʃiz/ **65**

cheek /tʃik/ **38**

cheese /tʃiz/ **63**

cheesecake /'tʃizkeɪk/ **66**

cheetah /'tʃitə/ **102**

chef /ʃɛf/ **27**

chemistry /'kɛməstri/ **59**

cherry /'tʃɛri/ **62**

chess /tʃɛs/ **95**

chessboard /'tʃɛsbɔrd/ **95**

chessman /'tʃɛsmæn/ **95**

chesspiece /'tʃɛspis/ **95**

chest /tʃɛst/ **37**

chest of drawers /ˌtʃɛst əv 'drɔrz/ **17**

chewing gum /'tʃuɪŋ ˌgʌm/ **83**

Cheyenne /ʃaɪ'yæn/ **8**

Chicago /ʃɪ'kɑgoʊ/ **8**

chick /tʃɪk/ **101**

chicken /'tʃɪkən/ **65, 101**

child /tʃaɪld/ **9**

children /'tʃɪldrən/ **10**

children's section /'tʃɪldrənz ˌsɛkʃən/ **60**

chilly /'tʃɪli/ **107**

chimney /'tʃɪmni/ **13**

chin /tʃɪn/ **37**

chipmunk /'tʃɪpmʌŋk/ **105**

chocolate /'tʃɑklɪt/ **83**

chocolate cake /'tʃɑklɪt 'keɪk/ **66**

chocolates /tʃɑklɪts/ **83**

chop /tʃɑp/ **69**

Christmas Day /ˌkrɪsməs 'deɪ/ **6**

Cincinnati /ˌsɪnsɪ'næti/ **8**

circle /'sɚkəl/ **5**

circumference /sɚ'kʌmfrəns/ **5**

clam /klæm/ **103**

clap /klæp/ **40**

clarinet /ˌklærə'nɛt/ **96**

classifieds /'klæsɪˌfaɪdz/ **26**

classroom /'klæsrum/ **56**

claw /klɔ/ **103, 104**

cleaning solution /'klinɪŋ səˈluʃən/ **48**

clear /klɪr/ **107**

Cleveland /'klivlənd/ **8**

cliff /klɪf/ **106**

climber /'klaɪmɚ/ **89**

clippers /'klɪpɚz/ **23**

clock /klɑk/ **7**

clock radio /ˌklɑk 'reɪdioʊ/ **110**

close /kloʊs/ **113**

closed /kloʊzd/ **114**

closet /'klɑzɪt/ **17**

clothesline /'kloʊzlaɪn/ **21**

clothespin /'kloʊzpɪn/ **21**

clothes rack /'kloʊz ræk/ **21**

clothing store /'kloʊðɪŋ ˌstɔr/ **84**

cloudy /'klaʊdi/ **107**

clutch /klʌtʃ/ **73**

clutch bag /'klʌtʃ bæg/ **55**

coastline /'koʊstlaɪn/ **106**

coat /koʊt/ **49**

Coast Guard boat /'koʊst gɑrd ˌboʊt/ **78**

cockatoo /'kɑkəˌtu/ **104**

cockpit /'kɑkˌpɪt/ **77**

cockroach /'kɑk-roʊtʃ/ **105**

cocoa /'koʊkoʊ/ **64**

coconut /'koʊkəˌnʌt/ **62**

coffee /'kɔfi/ **64, 66, 70**

coffee maker /'kɔfi ˌmeɪkɚ/ **15**

coffee table /'kɔfi ˌteɪbəl/ **18**

coin /kɔɪn/ **94**

coin collecting /'kɔɪn kəˌlɛktɪŋ/ **94**

coinslot /'kɔɪnslɑt/ **85**

colander /'kɑləndɚ/ **15**

cold /'koʊld/ **44, 107**

cold medicine /'koʊld ˌmɛdəsən/ **44**

coleslaw /'koʊlslɔ/ **65**

collar /'kɑlɚ/ **52**

collection /kə'lɛkʃən/ **82**

college /'kɑlɪdʒ/ **56**

cologne /kə'loʊn/ **43**

Colorado /ˌkɑlə'rɑdoʊ/ **8**

colored pen /ˌkʌlɚd 'pɛn/ **83**

coloring book /'kʌlərɪŋ ˌbʊk/ **57, 83**

colors /'kʌlɚz/ **53**

comb your hair /ˌkoʊm yɚ 'hɛr/ **12**

comb /koʊm/ **42, 43**

comet /'kɑmɪt/ **108**

comforter /'kʌmfɚtɚ/ **17**

compact disc /ˌkɑmpækt 'dɪsk/ **110**

compact disc player /ˌkɑmpækt 'dɪsk ˌpleɪɚ/ **110**

compartment /kəm'pɑrtˈmənt/ **77**

compass /'kʌmpəs/ **58**

compost /'kɑmpoʊst/ **23**

computer /kəm'pyutɚ/ **56, 60, 110**

computer games /kəm'pyutɚ ˌgeɪmz/ **95**

computer lab /kəm'pyutɚ ˌlæb/ **58**

computer technician /kəm'pyutɚ tɛkˌnɪʃən/ **29**

concert /'kɑnsɚt/ **93**

Concord /'kɑŋkɚd/ **8**

condiments /'kɑndəmənts/ **64**

conduct a meeting /kənˌdʌkt ə 'mitɪŋ/ **31**

conductor /kən'dʌktɚ/ **93**

cone /koʊn/ **75**

confectionery /kən'fɛkʃəˌnɛri/ **83**

conference room /'kɑnfrəns ˌrum/ **35**

confused /kən'fyuzd/ **113**

Connecticut /kə'nɛtɪkət/ **8**

constellation /ˌkɑnstə'leɪʃən/ **108**

construction site /kən'strʌkʃən ˌsaɪt/ **34**

construction worker /kən'strʌkʃən ˌwɚkɚ/ **34**

contact lenses /ˌkɑntækt 'lɛnzɪz/ **48**

control tower /kən'troʊl ˌtaʊɚ/ **77**

convertible /kən'vɚtəbəl/ **72**

conveyer belt /kən'veɪyɚ bɛlt/ **33, 63**

cook /kʊk/ **27**

cookbook /'kʊkbʊk/ **14**

cookies /'kʊkiz/ **64**

cookie sheet /'kʊki ˌʃit/ **15**

cooking /'kʊkɪŋ/ **69**

cool /kul/ **107**

cooler /'kulɚ/ **97**

copilot /'koʊˌpaɪlət/ **77**

cordless phone /ˌkɔrdlɪs 'foʊn/ **111**

corn /kɔrn/ **63**

corner /'kɔrnɚ/ **5**

corn on the cob /ˌkɔrn ɔn ðə 'kɑb/ **61**

cosmetics /kɑz'mɛtɪks/ **43**

cotton /'kɑtˈn/ **54**

couch /kaʊtʃ/ **18**

cough /kɔf/ **44**

cough syrup /'kɔf ˌsɚəp/ **44**

counselor /'kaʊnsəlɚ/ **46**

counter /'kaʊntɚ/ **82**

counter top /'kaʊntɚ ˌtɑp/ **14**

countryside /'kʌntriˌsaɪd/ **98**

couple /'kʌpəl/ **9**

court /kɔrt/ **87, 88**

court reporter /ˌkɔrt rɪ'pɔrtɚ/ **36**

courtroom /'kɔrtˈrum/ **36**

cousins /'kʌzənz/ **11**

cover letter /'kʌvɚ ˌlɛtɚ/ **26**

cow /kaʊ/ **101**

crab /kræb/ **65, 103**

craft fair /'kræft fɛr/ **99**

crane /kreɪn/ **34, 78, 104**

crayon /'kreɪɑn/ **57**

cream /krim/ **45, 53**

cream cheese /ˌkrim 'tʃiz/ **70**

credit card /'krɛdɪt ˌkɑrd/ **79**

crescent moon /ˌkrɛsənt 'mun/ **108**

crest /krɛst/ **104**

crewneck sweater /ˌkrunɛk 'swɛtɚ/ **49**

crib /krɪb/ **20**

crime /kraɪm/ **36**

crocodile /'krɑkəˌdaɪl/ **102**

croissant /krwɑ'sɑnt/ **70**

cross-country skiing /ˌkrɔs kʌntri 'ski-ɪŋ/ **91**

crosswalk /'krɔswɔk/ **74, 80**

crow /kroʊ/ **104**

crowd /kraʊd/ **86**

cruise ship /'kruz ʃɪp/ **78**

crush /krʌʃ/ **69**

crutches /'krʌtʃɪz/ **47**

cry /kraɪ/ **40**

cube /kyub/ **5**

cucumbers /'kyuˌkʌmbɚz/ **61**

cuff /kʌf/ **52**

cuff link /'kʌf lɪŋk/ **55**

cup /kʌp/ **16, 19, 68**

cupboard /'kʌbɚd/ **14**

cupcake /'kʌpkeɪk/ **65**

curb /kɚb/ **80**

curly hair /ˌkɚli 'hɛr/ **39**

cursor /'kɚsɚ/ **109**

curtains /'kɚtˈnz/ **17**

cushion /'kʊʃən/ **18**

customer /'kʌstəmɚ/ **63, 79, 82**

customs /'kʌstəmz/ **76**

customs officer /'kʌstəmz ˌɔfəsɚ/ **76**

cut /kʌt/ **41, 42, 45**

cutlery /'kʌtləri/ **19**
cutting board /ˌkʌtɪŋ ˌbɔrd/ **15**
cycling /'saɪklɪŋ/ **89**
cyclist /'saɪklɪst/ **89**
cylinder /'sɪləndɚ/ **5**
cylinder block /'sɪləndɚ ˌblɑk/ **72**
cymbal /'sɪmbəl/ **96**

daffodil /'dæfəˌdɪl/ **22**
Dallas /'dæləs/ **8**
daily planner /ˌdeɪli 'plænɚ/ **55**
dairy products /'dɛri ˌprɑdʌkts/ **63**
daisy /'deɪzi/ **22**
dam /ˌdæm/ **106**
dance /dæns/ **40**
dark /dɑrk/ **114**
dark blue /ˌdɑrk 'blu/ **53**
dark green /ˌdɑrk 'grin/ **53**
dark hair /ˌdɑrk 'hɛr/ **39**
dashboard /'dæʃbɔrd/ **73**
date /deɪt/ **62**
datebook /'deɪtˌbʊk/ **30**
daughter /'dɔtɚ/ **10**
daughter-in-law /'dɔtɚ ɪn ˌlɔ/ **11**
days of the week /ˌdeɪz əv ðə 'wik/ **6**
debit card /'dɛbɪt ˌkɑrd/ **79**
December /dɪ'sɛmbɚ/ **6**
deck /dɛk/ **78**
deep /dip/ **114**
deer /dɪr/ **102**
defense attorney /dɪ'fɛns əˌtɚni/ **36**
defendant /dɪ'fɛndənt/ **36**
Delaware /'dɛləˌwɛr/ **8**
deli /'dɛli/ **65**
delicatessen /ˌdɛlikə'tɛsən/ **65**
delivery /dɪ'lɪvri/ **82**
denim /'dɛnəm/ **54**
dental assistant /'dɛntl əˌsɪstənt/ **48**
dental care /'dɛntl ˌkɛr/ **48**
dental floss /'dɛntl ˌflɔs/ **48**
dental hygienist /ˌdɛntl haɪ'dʒɪnɪst/ **48**
dentist /'dɛntɪst/ **28, 48**
dentures /'dɛntʃɚz/ **48**
Denver /'dɛnvɚ/ **8**
department store /dɪ'pɑrtˌmənt ˌstɔr/ **80**
departure lounge /dɪ'pɑrtʃɚ ˌlaʊndʒ/ **76**
depth /dɛpθ/ **5**
desert /'dɛzɚt/ **106**
designer /dɪ'zaɪnɚ/ **29**
desk /dɛsk/ **18, 30, 56**
desk calendar /'dɛsk ˌkæləndɚ/ **30**

desk clerk /'dɛsk klɚk/ **35**
desk lamp /'dɛsk læmp/ **30**
dessert /dɪ'zɚt/ **66**
dessert cart /dɪ'zɚt ˌkɑrt/ **66**
Detroit /dɪ'trɔɪt/ **8**
diagonal /daɪ'ægənəl/ **5**
diameter /daɪ'æmətɚ/ **5**
diamond /'daɪmənd/ **55**
diaper /'daɪpɚ/ **20**
dice /daɪs/ **95**
dictionary /'dɪkʃəˌnɛri/ **60**
digital camera /ˌdɪdʒɪtl 'kæmrə/ **111**
digital watch /ˌdɪdʒɪtl 'wɑtʃ/ **7**
dig the soil /ˌdɪg ðə 'sɔɪl/ **23**
dime /daɪm/ **79**
dining room /'daɪnɪŋ ˌrum/ **19**
dining room table /ˌdaɪnɪŋ rum 'teɪbəl/ **19**
dip /dɪp/ **65**
dish /dɪʃ/ **19**
dishwasher /'dɪʃˌwɑʃɚ/ **14**
dishwashing liquid /'dɪʃwɑʃɪŋ ˌlɪkwɪd/ **14**
diskette /dɪ'skɛt/ **109**
distributor /dɪ'strɪbyətɚ/ **72**
diver /'daɪvɚ/ **90**
divided by /də'vaɪdɪd baɪ/ **4**
divider /də'vaɪdɚ/ **74**
diving board /'daɪvɪŋ ˌbɔrd/ **90**
diving /'daɪvɪŋ/ **90**
divorced /də'vɔrst/ **9**
dock /dɑk/ **78**
doctor /'dɑktɚ/ **28, 46, 47**
doctor's office /'dɑktɚz ˌɔfɪs/ **46**
document /'dɑkyəmənt/ **109**
dog /dɔg/ **100**
doghouse /'dɔghaʊs/ **100**
do homework /ˌdu 'hoʊmwɚk/ **25**
doll /dɑl/ **57**
dollar bill /ˌdɑlɚ 'bɪl/ **79**
dollar coin /ˌdɑlɚ ˌkɔɪn/ **79**
dolly /'dɑli/ **33**
dolphin /'dɑlfɪn/ **103**
do not enter sign /ˌdu nɑt 'ɛntɚ ˌsaɪn/ **75**
donut /'doʊnʌt/ **67**
donkey /'dɑŋki/ **101**
don't walk sign /ˌdoʊnt 'wɔk ˌsaɪn/ **80**
door /dɔr/ **73**
doorbell /'dɔrbɛl/ **13**
doorknob /'dɔrnɑb/ **13**
do push-ups /ˌdu 'pʊʃʌps/ **92**
do sit-ups /ˌdu 'sɪtʌps/ **92**
do the laundry /ˌdu ðə 'lɔndri/ **25**
double bass /ˌdʌbəl 'beɪs/ **96**
double bed /ˌdʌbəl 'bɛd/ **17**

double room /ˌdʌbəl 'rum/ **35**
double yellow line /ˌdʌbəl ˌyɛloʊ 'laɪn/ **80**
doughnut /'doʊnʌt/ **67**
down /daʊn/ **115**
downhill skiing /ˌdaʊnhɪl 'ski-ɪŋ/ **91**
dragonfly /'drægənˌflaɪ/ **105**
drainpipe /'dreɪnpaɪp/ **13**
drama /'drɑmə/ **59**
drape /dreɪp/ **18**
draw /drɔ/ **41**
drawer /drɔr/ **17**
dress /drɛs/ **50**
dresser /'drɛsɚ/ **17**
dressing table /'drɛsɪŋ ˌteɪbəl/ **17**
dressmaker /'drɛsˌmeɪkɚ/ **54**
drill /drɪl/ **48**
drill bit /'drɪl bɪt/ **32**
drinks /drɪŋks/ **64, 66**
driveway /'draɪvweɪ/ **13**
drugstore /'drʌgstɔr/ **84**
drum /drʌm/ **96**
drum set /'drʌm sɛt/ **96**
drummer /'drʌmɚ/ **93**
dry /draɪ/ **114**
dry goods /'draɪ gʊdz/ **64**
dry your face /ˌdraɪ yɚ 'feɪs/ **12**
dry yourself /'draɪ yɚˌsɛlf/ **12**
duck /dʌk/ **101**
duckling /'dʌklɪŋ/ **101**
dump truck /'dʌmp trʌk/ **34**
duplex /'duplɛks/ **13**
dust /dʌst/ **25**
dustcloth /'dʌstklɔθ/ **21**
dustpan /'dʌstpæn/ **21**
dust ruffle /'dʌst ˌrʌfəl/ **17**
duty-free shop /ˌduti 'fri ˌʃɑp/ **76**
DVD /ˌdi vi 'di/ **110**
DVD player /ˌdi vi 'di ˌpleɪɚ/ **110**

eagle /'igəl/ **104**
ear /ɪr/ **37**
ear protectors /'ɪr prəˌtɛktɚz/ **34**
earring /'ɪrɪŋ/ **55**
Earth /ɚθ/ **108**
easel /'izəl/ **57**
east /ist/ **8**
East Coast /ˌist 'koʊst/ **8**
Easter /'istɚ/ **6**
eat breakfast /ˌit 'brɛkfəst/ **12**
edge /ɛdʒ/ **5**
eel /il/ **103**
egg /ɛg/ **63, 104**
egg beaters /'ɛg ˌbitɚz/ **15**
eggplant /'ɛgplænt/ **61**
eight /eɪt/ **4**

eighteen /ˌeɪ'tin/ **4**
eighty /'eɪti/ **4**
elbow /'ɛlboʊ/ **37**
elbow pads /'ɛlboʊ ˌpædz/ **89**
electric drill /ɪˌlɛktrɪk 'drɪl/ **32**
electric guitar /ɪˌlɛktrɪk gɪ'tɑr/ **96**
electrical outlet /ɪˌlɛktrɪkəl 'aʊtˌlɛt/ **21**
electrician /ɪˌlɛk'trɪʃən/ **27**
electric mixer /ɪˌlɛktrɪk 'mɪksɚ/ **15**
electric shaver /ɪˌlɛktrɪk 'ʃeɪvɚ/ **43**
electronic personal organizer /ɪlɛkˌtrɑnɪk ˌpɚsənəl 'ɔrgənaɪzɚ/ **111**
electronics store /ɪlɛk'trɑnɪks ˌstɔr/ **84**
elementary school /ɛlə'mɛntri ˌskul/ **56**
elephant /'ɛləfənt/ **102**
elevator /'ɛləˌveɪtɚ/ **35**
eleven /ɪ'lɛvən/ **4**
ellipse /ɪ'lɪps/ **5**
El Paso /ɛl 'pæsoʊ/ **8**
embroidery /ɪm'brɔɪdəri/ **94**
emerald /'ɛmərəld/ **55**
emergency brake /ɪ'mɚdʒənsi 'breɪk/ **73**
emergency number /ɪ'mɚdʒənsi ˌnʌmbɚ/ **85**
emery board /'ɛmri ˌbɔrd/ **43**
empty /'ɛmpti/ **68, 113**
encyclopedia /ɪnˌsaɪklə'pidiə/ **60**
engine /'ɛndʒɪn/ **71, 72**
English literature /ˌɪŋglɪʃ 'lɪtərətʃɚ/ **59**
ENT specialist /ˌi ɛn 'ti ˌspɛʃəlɪst/ **46**
envelope /'ɛnvəˌloʊp/ **82**
equals /'ikwəlz/ **4**
eraser /ɪ'reɪsɚ/ **30, 58, 83**
escalator /'ɛskəˌleɪtɚ/ **71, 84**
evening /'ivnɪŋ/ **7**
evening gown /'ivnɪŋ ˌgaʊn/ **50**
evidence /'ɛvədəns/ **36**
examination table /ɪgzæmə'neɪʃən ˌteɪbəl/ **46**
excavation site /ɛkskə'veɪʃən ˌsaɪt/ **34**
excited /ɪk'saɪtɪd/ **113**
exercise bike /'ɛksɚsaɪz ˌbaɪk/ **92**
exhaust pipe /ɪg'zɔst ˌpaɪp/ **73**
exhibition /ˌɛksə'bɪʃən/ **99**
exit /'ɛgzɪt/ **74**
ex-husband /ˌɛks 'hʌzbənd/ **10**
expensive /ɪk'spɛnsɪv/ **114**
ex-wife /ˌɛks 'waɪf/ **10**
eye /aɪ/ **37**

grape /greɪp/ **62**

grapefruit /ˈgreɪpfrut/ **62, 70**

grass /græs/ **106**

grasshopper /ˈgræsˌhɑpə/ **105**

grate /greɪt/ **69**

grater /ˈgreɪtə/ **15**

gray /greɪ/ **53**

grease /gris/ **69**

Great Salt Lake /ˌgreɪt sɑlt ˈleɪk/ **8**

green /grin/ **89**

green beans /ˌgrin ˈbinz/ **61**

green light /ˌgrin ˈlaɪt/ **74**

green onions /ˌgrin ˈʌnyənz/ **61**

green pepper /ˌgrin ˈpɛpə/ **61**

greet visitors /ˌgrit ˈvɪzɪtəz/ **31**

grill /grɪl/ **69**

groceries /ˈgroʊʃəriz/ **63**

grocery clerk /ˈgroʊʃəri ˌklək/ **27**

ground beef /ˌgraʊnd ˈbif/ **65**

ground cloth /ˈgraʊnd klɔθ/ **98**

groundhog /ˈgraʊndhɑg/ **105**

guard /gɑrd/ **86**

guest /gɛst/ **35**

Gulf of Mexico /ˌgʌlf əv ˈmɛksɪkoʊ/ **8**

guinea pig /ˈgɪni ˌpɪg/ **100**

guitarist /gɪˈtɑrɪst/ **93**

gums /gʌmz/ **48**

gurney /ˈgəni/ **47**

gutter /ˈgʌtə/ **13, 80, 88**

gym /dʒɪm/ **58, 59**

gymnast /ˈdʒɪmnəst/ **89**

gymnastics /dʒɪmˈnæstɪks/ **89**

gynecologist /ˌgaɪnəˈkɑlədʒɪst/ **46**

hair /hɛr/ **37**

hairbrush /ˈhɛrbrʌʃ/ **42**

hairdresser /ˈhɛrˌdrɛsə/ **29, 42**

hairdresser's chair /ˈhɛrdrɛsəz ˌtʃɛr/ **42**

hairdryer /ˈhɛrˌdraɪə/ **42, 43**

half full /ˌhæf ˈfʊl/ **68**

half moon /ˌhæf ˈmun/ **108**

Halloween /ˌhæləˈwin/ **6**

hallway /ˈhɔlweɪ/ **24**

ham /hæm/ **65**

hamburger /ˈhæmˌbəgə/ **67**

hammer /ˈhæmə/ **32**

hamper /ˈhæmpə/ **16**

hamster /ˈhæmstə/ **100**

hand /hænd/ **37**

handbag /ˈhændbæg/ **55**

handcuffs /ˈhændkʌfs/ **36**

handkerchief /ˈhæŋkətʃif/ **55**

handle /ˈhændl/ **15**

hand mirror /ˈhænd ˌmɪrə/ **42**

handrail /ˈhændreɪl/ **80**

handset /ˈhændsɛt/ **111**

hand towel /ˈhænd ˌtaʊəl/ **16**

hangar /ˈhæŋə/ **77**

hanger /ˈhæŋə/ **21**

happy /ˈhæpi/ **113**

hard /hɑrd/ **114**

hard drive /ˌhɑrd ˌdraɪv/ **109**

hard hat /ˈhɑrd hæt/ **34**

hardware /ˈhɑrdwɛr/ **109**

harmonica /hɑrˈmɑnɪkə/ **96**

harness /ˈhɑrnɪs/ **89**

hat /hæt/ **49**

hatchback /ˈhætʃbæk/ **72**

have a cup of coffee /ˌhæv ə ˌkʌp əv ˈkɔfi/ **12**

Hawaii /həˈwaɪ-i/ **8**

hazelnut /ˈheɪzəlˌnʌt/ **62**

hazy /ˈheɪzi/ **107**

head /hɛd/ **37**

headache /ˈhɛdeɪk/ **44**

headboard /ˈhɛdbɔrd/ **17**

headlight /ˈhɛdlaɪt/ **73**

headphones /ˈhɛdfoʊnz/ **58, 110**

headrest /ˈhɛdrɛst/ **73**

heart /hɑrt/ **38**

heavy /ˈhɛvi/ **39, 113**

hedge /hɛdʒ/ **22**

heel /hil/ **37, 52**

height /haɪt/ **5**

height chart /ˈhaɪt tʃɑrt/ **46**

Helena /ˈhɛlənə/ **8**

helicopter /ˈhɛliˌkɑptə/ **77**

helmet /ˈhɛlmɪt/ **86, 89, 91**

hemline /ˈhɛmlaɪn/ **52**

herbs /əbz/ **64**

hi-fi /ˌhaɪ ˈfaɪ/ **110**

high chair /ˈhaɪ tʃɛr/ **20**

high school /ˈhaɪ skul/ **56**

high-rise building /ˌhaɪ raɪz ˈbɪldɪŋ/ **81**

highlights /ˈhaɪlaɪts/ **42**

highway /ˈhaɪweɪ/ **74**

hiker /ˈhaɪkə/ **98**

hiking /ˈhaɪkɪŋ/ **98**

hill /hɪl/ **106**

hip /hɪp/ **37**

hip-bone /ˈhɪp boʊn/ **38**

hippopotamus /ˌhɪpəˈpɑtəməs/ **102**

historic battlefield /hɪˌstɔrɪk ˈbætlfild/ **99**

hobby /ˈhɑbi/ **94**

hold /hoʊld/ **41**

hole /hoʊl/ **89**

hole puncher /ˈhoʊl ˌpʌntʃə/ **30**

holidays /ˈhɑləˌdeɪz/ **6**

home /hoʊm/ **25**

home economics /ˌhoʊm ɛkəˈnɑmɪks/ **59**

home plate /ˌhoʊm ˈpleɪt/ **86**

honey /ˈhʌni/ **63**

honeycomb /ˈhʌniˌkoʊm/ **105**

honeydew melon /ˈhʌnidu ˌmɛlən/ **62**

hood /hʊd/ **52, 73**

hook /hʊk/ **32, 34**

hook and eye /ˌhʊk ən ˈaɪ/ **54**

hoop /hup/ **87**

hop /hɑp/ **92**

horn /hɔrn/ **102**

hors d'oeuvres /ɔr ˈdəvz/ **66**

horse /hɔrs/ **89, 101**

horseback riding /ˈhɔrsbæk ˌraɪdɪŋ/ **89**

horse racing /ˈhɔrs ˌreɪsɪŋ/ **87**

hose /hoʊz/ **23, 72, 85**

hospital /ˈhɑspɪtl/ **47**

hospital ward /ˈhɑspɪtl ˌwɔrd/ **47**

hot /hɑt/ **107**

hot-air balloon /ˌhɑt ˈɛr bəˌlun/ **98**

hot cereal /ˌhɑt ˈsɪriəl/ **70**

hotdog /ˈhɑtdɔg/ **67**

hotel /hoʊˈtɛl/ **35**

hour hand /ˈaʊə hænd/ **7**

house /haʊs/ **13**

household products /ˌhaʊshoʊld ˈprɑdʌkts/ **64**

housekeeper /ˈhaʊsˌkipə/ **35**

Houston /ˈhyustən/ **8**

hubcap /ˈhʌbkæp/ **73**

hug /hʌg/ **40**

hummingbird /ˈhʌmɪŋˌbəd/ **104**

hump /hʌmp/ **102**

hurt /hət/ **45**

husband /ˈhʌzbənd/ **10**

hutch /hʌtʃ/ **100**

hyacinth /ˈhaɪəˌsɪnθ/ **22**

hypotenuse /haɪˈpɑtⁿ-us/ **5**

ice /aɪs/ **91**

ice cream /ˈaɪs krim/ **66, 67**

ice cream cone /ˈaɪs krim ˌkoʊn/ **67**

ice skate /ˈaɪs skeɪt/ **91**

icon /ˈaɪkɑn/ **109**

icy /ˈaɪsi/ **107**

Idaho /ˈaɪdəˌhoʊ/ **8**

Illinois /ˌɪləˈnɔɪ/ **8**

immigration and naturalization /ˌɪməˌgreɪʃən ən nætʃrələˈzeɪʃən/ **76**

immigration officer /ˌɪməˈgreɪʃən ˌɔfəsə/ **76**

in /ɪn/ **115**

in box /ˈɪn bɑks/ **30**

Independence Day /ˌɪndəˈpɛndəns ˌdeɪ/ **6**

Indiana /ˌɪndiˈænə/ **8**

Indianapolis /ˌɪndiəˈnæpəlɪs/ **8**

infield /ˈɪnfild/ **86**

information desk /ɪnfəˈmeɪʃən ˌdɛsk/ **60**

in front of /ɪn ˈfrʌnt əv/ **115**

in-laws /ˈɪn lɔz/ **11**

in-line skate /ˌɪn laɪn ˈskeɪt/ **89**

inmate /ˈɪnmeɪt/ **36**

insect bite /ˈɪnsɛkt ˌbaɪt/ **45**

insect repellent /ˈɪnsɛkt rɪˈpɛlənt/ **45**

insect /ˈɪnsɛkt/ **105**

inside /ɪnˈsaɪd/ **116**

instrument panel /ˈɪnstrəmənt ˌpænl/ **77**

intercom /ˈɪntəˌkɑm/ **13, 20**

intersection /ˈɪntəˌsɛkʃən/ **74**

interstate highway sign /ˌɪntəsteɪt ˈhaɪweɪ ˌsaɪn/ **75**

interviewer /ˈɪntəˌvyuə/ **26**

in the middle of /ɪn ðə ˈmɪdl əv/ **116**

into /ˈɪntu/ **116**

intravenous drip /ˌɪntrəvinəs ˈdrɪp/ **85**

Iowa /ˈaɪəwə/ **8**

iron /ˈaɪən/ **21, 25**

ironing board /ˈaɪənɪŋ ˌbɔrd/ **21**

iron the clothes /ˌaɪən ðə ˈkloʊz/ **25**

iron-on tape /ˌaɪən ɑn ˈteɪp/ **54**

island /ˈaɪlənd/ **106**

isosceles triangle /aɪˌsɑsəliz ˈtraɪæŋgəl/ **5**

jacket /ˈdʒækɪt/ **49, 50, 51**

jackhammer /ˈdʒækˌhæmə/ **34**

Jackson /ˈdʒæksən/ **8**

Jacksonville /ˈdʒæksənvɪl/ **8**

jail /dʒeɪl/ **36**

jam /dʒæm/ **70**

January /ˈdʒænyuˌɛri/ **6**

jar /dʒɑr/ **68**

jeans /dʒinz/ **50, 51**

jelly /ˈdʒɛli/ **63, 70**

jellyfish /ˈdʒɛliˌfɪʃ/ **103**

jet /dʒɛt/ **77**

jewelry /ˈdʒuəlri/ **55**

jigsaw puzzle /ˈdʒɪgsɔ ˌpʌzəl/ **57**

job announcement board /ˈdʒɑb əˌnaʊnsmənt ˌbɔrd/ **26**

job candidate /ˈdʒɑb ˌkændədɪt/ **26**

job interview /ˈdʒɑb ˌɪntəvyu/ **26**

jobs /dʒɑbz/ **27**

jockey /ˈdʒɑki/ **87**

jockey shorts /ˈdʒɑki ˌʃɔrts/ **51**

jogger /ˈdʒɑgə/ **89**

journalist /ˈdʒənl-ɪst/ **29**

judge /dʒʌdʒ/ **28, 36**
judo /'dʒudoʊ/ **88**
juice /dʒus/ **64**
July /dʒʊ'laɪ/ **6**
jump /'dʒʌmp/ **92**
jump rope /'dʒʌmp roʊp/ **92**
June /dʒun/ **6**
jungle gym /ˌdʒʌŋgəl 'dʒɪm/ **57**
junior high school /ˌdʒunyɚ 'haɪ skul/ **56**
Jupiter /'dʒupɪtɚ/ **108**
jury /'dʒʊri/ **36**

kangaroo /ˌkæŋgə'ru/ **102**
Kansas /'kænzəs/ **8**
Kansas City /ˌkænzəs 'sɪt̮i/ **8**
karate /kə'rɑt̮i/ **88**
Kentucky /kən'tʌki/ **8**
ketchup /'kɛtʃəp/ **64**
kettle /'kɛt̮l/ **15**
key ring /'ki rɪŋ/ **55**
keyboard /'kibɔrd/ **58, 96, 109**
keypad /'kipæd/ **111**
kick /kɪk/ **92**
kid /kɪd/ **101**
kidney /'kɪdni/ **38**
killer whale /ˌkɪlɚ 'weɪl/ **103**
kindergarten /'kɪndɚˌgɑrt⌐n/ **56**
kiss /kɪs/ **40**
kite /kaɪt/ **57**
kitten /'kɪt⌐n/ **100**
kiwi /'kiwi/ **62**
knead /nid/ **69**
knee /ni/ **37**
kneecap /'nikæp/ **38**
kneel /nil/ **92**
knife /naɪf/ **15, 19**
knitting /'nɪt̮ɪŋ/ **54, 94**
knitting needle /'nɪt̮ɪŋ ˌnidl/ **54, 94**
knob /nɑb/ **17**
knocker /'nɑkɚ/ **13**
koala bear /koʊ'ɑlə ˌbɛr/ **102**

ladder /'lædɚ/ **34, 85**
ladle /'leɪdl/ **15**
ladybug /'leɪdiˌbʌg/ **105**
lake /leɪk/ **98, 106**
Lake Erie /ˌleɪk 'ɪri/ **8**
Lake Huron /ˌleɪk 'hyʊrɑn/ **8**
Lake Michigan /ˌleɪk 'mɪʃɪgən/ **8**
Lake Ontario /ˌleɪk ɑn'tɛrioʊ/ **8**
Lake Superior /ˌleɪk sə'pɪriɚ/ **8**
lamb /læm/ **101**
lamb chops /'læm ˌtʃɑps/ **65**
lamp /læmp/ **17, 18, 48**
lampshade /'læmpʃeɪd/ **18**
landing /'lændɪŋ/ **77**
lane /leɪn/ **74, 88**
language lab /'læŋgwɪdʒ ˌlæb/ **58**
languages /'læŋgwɪdʒɪz/ **59**
lapel /lə'pɛl/ **52**
laptop /'læptɑp/ **109**
large intestine /ˌlɑrdʒ ɪn'tɛstɪn/ **38**
lasagna /lə'zɑnyə/ **66**
Las Vegas /lɑs 'veɪgəs/ **8**
laugh /læf/ **40**
launch pad /'lɔntʃ pæd/ **108**
laundry basket /'lɔndri ˌbæskɪt/ **16, 21**
laundry detergent /'lɔndri dɪˌtɚdʒənt/ **21**
lawn /lɔn/ **22**
lawn mower /'lɔn ˌmoʊɚ/ **23**
lawyer /'lɔyɚ/ **28**
leather /'lɛðɚ/ **54**
lecturer /'lɛktʃərɚ/ **28**
leeks /liks/ **61**
leg /lɛg/ **37**
leg of lamb /ˌlɛg əv 'læm/ **65**
lemon /'lɛmən/ **62**
length /lɛŋkθ/ **5**
lens /lɛnz/ **48, 111**
leopard /'lɛpɚd/ **102**
letter /'lɛt̮ɚ/ **82**
letter carrier /'lɛt̮ɚ ˌkæriɚ/ **82**
lettuce /'lɛt̮ɪs/ **61**
level /'lɛvəl/ **34**
librarian /laɪ'brɛriən/ **60**
library /'laɪˌbrɛri/ **60**
library card /'laɪbrɛri ˌkɑrd/ **60**
license plate /'laɪsəns ˌpleɪt/ **73**
lid /lɪd/ **15**
lie down /ˌlaɪ 'daʊn/ **40**
lifeguard /'laɪfgɑrd/ **97**
life jacket /'laɪf ˌdʒækɪt/ **77, 78**
lift /lɪft/ **92**
light /laɪt/ **113**
light bulb /'laɪt⌐ bʌlb/ **111**
light hair /ˌlaɪt 'hɛr/ **39**
lighthouse /'laɪthaʊs/ **78**
lightning /'laɪt⌐nɪŋ/ **107**
lime /laɪm/ **62**
linen /'lɪnən/ **54**
lines /laɪnz/ **5**
lion /'laɪən/ **102**
lips /lɪps/ **37**
lipstick /'lɪpˌstɪk/ **43**
listen to the radio /ˌlɪsən tə ðə 'reɪdioʊ/ **12**
Little Rock /'lɪt̮l ˌrɑk/ **8**
liver /'lɪvɚ/ **38, 65**
living room /'lɪvɪŋ ˌrum/ **18**
lizard /'lɪzɚd/ **102**
llama /'lɑmə/ **102**
loading dock /'loʊdɪŋ ˌdɑk/ **33**
load the dishwasher /ˌloʊd ðə 'dɪʃwɑʃɚ/ **25**
loaf /loʊf/ **68**
lobby /'lɑbi/ **35**
lobster /'lɑbstɚ/ **65, 103**
lollipop /'lɑliˌpɑp/ **83**
long /lɔŋ/ **114**
long hair /ˌlɔŋ 'hɛr/ **39**
long-sleeved /ˌlɔŋ 'slivd/ **52**
loose /lus/ **52, 113**
Los Angeles /lɔs 'ændʒələs/ **8**
Louisiana /lʊˌizi'ænə/ **8**
Louisville /'luivɪl/ **8**
lounge chair /'laʊndʒ tʃɛr/ **22**
luggage /'lʌgɪdʒ/ **76**
luggage carousel /'lʌgɪdʒ ˌkærəˌsɛl/ **76**
luggage cart /'lʌgɪdʒ ˌkɑrt/ **76**
luggage compartment /'lʌgɪdʒ kəmˌpɑrt⌐mənt/ **71**
lunar module /ˌlunɚ 'mɑdʒul/ **108**
lunar vehicle /ˌlunɚ 'viikəl/ **108**
lunchmeat /'lʌntʃmit/ **65**
lung /lʌŋ/ **38**

machine /mə'ʃin/ **33**
mad /mæd/ **113**
magazine /ˌmægə'zin/ **60, 83**
magazine stand /ˌmægə'zin stænd/ **81**
magnifying glass /'mægnəfaɪ-ɪŋ ˌglæs/ **94**
maid /meɪd/ **35**
mail /meɪl/ **82**
mailbag /'meɪlbæg/ **82**
mailbox /'meɪlbɑks/ **13, 82**
mail carrier /'meɪl ˌkæriɚ/ **28, 82**
mail truck /'meɪl trʌk/ **82**
mail van /'meɪl væn/ **82**
main course /ˌmeɪn 'kɔrs/ **66**
Maine /meɪn/ **8**
make a sandwich /ˌmeɪk ə 'sændwɪtʃ/ **25**
make breakfast /ˌmeɪk 'brɛkfəst/ **25**
make dinner /ˌmeɪk 'dɪnɚ/ **25**
make lunch /ˌmeɪk 'lʌntʃ/ **25**
make the bed /ˌmeɪk ðə 'bɛd/ **25**
make-up /'meɪkʌp/ **43**
make-up bag /'meɪkʌp ˌbæg/ **55**
man /mæn/ **9**
mane /meɪn/ **102**
mango /'mæŋgoʊ/ **62**
manhole /'mænhoʊl/ **81**
manhole cover /'mænhoʊl ˌkʌvɚ/ **81**
manicure items /'mænɪˌkyʊr ˌaɪt̮əm/ **43**
mantelpiece /'mænt̮lˌpis/ **18**
March /mɑrtʃ/ **6**
margarine /'mɑrdʒərɪn/ **63**
marina /mə'rinə/ **78**
married /'mærɪd/ **9**
married couple /ˌmærɪd 'kʌpəl/ **10**
Mars /mɑrz/ **108**
martial arts /'mɑrʃəl/ **88**
Maryland /'mɛrələnd/ **8**
mascara /mæ'skærə/ **43**
mask /mæsk/ **47, 86, 90**
Massachusetts /ˌmæsə'tʃusɪts/ **8**
massage /mə'sɑʒ/ **42**
mast /mæst/ **90**
mat /mæt/ **58, 88, 92**
matches /'mætʃɪz/ **83**
math /mæθ/ **59**
mattress /'mætrɪs/ **17**
May /meɪ/ **6**
mayonnaise /'meɪəˌneɪz/ **64**
meadow /'mɛdoʊ/ **106**
measure /'mɛʒɚ/ **69**
measuring cup /'mɛʒərɪŋ ˌkʌp/ **15**
measuring spoons /'mɛʒərɪŋ spunz/ **15**
meat /mit/ **65**
mechanic /mɪ'kænɪk/ **27**
medical care /'mɛdɪkəl ˌkɛr/ **46**
medical records /ˌmɛdɪkəl 'rɛkɚdz/ **46**
medical specialist /ˌmɛdɪkəl 'spɛʃəlɪst/ **46**
medicine cabinet /'mɛdəsən ˌkæbənɪt/ **16**
Memorial Day /mə'mɔriəl ˌdeɪ/ **6**
Memphis /'mɛmfɪs/ **8**
menu /'mɛnyu/ **66**
men's wear /mɛnz wɛr/ **49**
Mercury /'mɚkyəri/ **108**
messy /'mɛsi/ **114**
metal /'mɛt̮l/ **55**
metal detector /'mɛt̮l dɪˌtɛktɚ/ **76**
meter /'mit̮ɚ/ **82**
Mexico /'mɛksɪˌkoʊ/ **8**
Miami /maɪ'æmi/ **8**
Michigan /'mɪʃɪgən/ **8**
microphone /'maɪkrəˌfoʊn/ **96**
microwave oven /ˌmaɪkrəweɪv 'ʌvən/ **14**
Mid-Atlantic /ˌmɪd ət'læntɪk/ **8**
midday /mɪd'deɪ/ **7**
middle school /'mɪdl ˌskul/ **56**
middle seat /'mɪdl ˌsit/ **77**
midnight /'mɪdnaɪt/ **7**
Midwest /ˌmɪd'wɛst/ **8**
mike /maɪk/ **96**
milk /mɪlk/ **63, 66, 70**
milkshake /'mɪlkʃeɪk/ **67**
Milwaukee /mɪl'wɔki/ **8**
mineral water /'mɪnərəl ˌwɔt̮ɚ/ **64**

minivan /'mɪni,væn/ **72**
Minneapolis /,mɪni'æpəlɪs/ **8**
Minnesota /,mɪnə'soʊṭə/ **8**
mints /mɪnts/ **83**
minus /'maɪnəs/ **4**
minute hand /'mɪnɪt ,hænd/ **7**
mirror /'mɪrɚ/ **16, 17, 19, 48**
missing button /,mɪsɪŋ 'bʌtˀn/ **54**
Mississippi /,mɪsə'sɪpi/ **8**
Missouri /mɪ'zʊri/ **8**
mitt /mɪt/ **86**
mix /mɪks/ **69**
mixing bowl /'mɪksɪŋ ,boʊl/ **15**
mobile phone /,moʊbəl 'foʊn/ **111**
model /'madl/ **29**
moisturizer /'mɔɪstʃə,raɪzɚ/ **43**
mole /moʊl/ **105**
Monday /'mʌndi/ **6**
money /'mʌni/ **79**
monitor /'manəṭɚ/ **109**
monkey /'mʌŋki/ **102**
Montana /man'tænə/ **8**
month /mʌnθ/ **6**
monument /'manyəmənt/ **99**
moon /mun/ **108**
mop /map/ **21**
mop the floor /,map ðə 'flɔr/ **25**
moped /'moʊpɛd/ **72**
morning /'mɔrnɪŋ/ **7**
mosquito /mə'skiṭoʊ/ **105**
moth /mɔθ/ **105**
mother /'mʌðɚ/ **10**
Mother's Day /'mʌðɚz ,deɪ/ **6**
mother-in-law /'mʌðɚ ɪn ,lɔ/ **11**
motorboat /'moʊṭɚ,boʊt/ **90**
motorcycle /'moʊṭɚ,saɪkəl/ **72**
motor home /,moʊṭɚ 'hoʊm/ **72**
motor scooter /'moʊṭɚ ,skuṭɚ/ **72**
mountain /'maʊntˀn/ **106**
mouse /maʊs/ **105, 109**
mouse pad /'maʊs pæd/ **109**
mouth /maʊθ/ **37**
movie screen /'muvi ,skrin/ **93**
movie theater /'muvi ,θiəṭɚ/ **93**
movies /'muviz/ **93**
mow the lawn /,moʊ ðə 'lɔn/ **23**
muffin /'mʌfən/ **67**
multiplied by /'mʌltə,plaɪd baɪ/ **4**
muscle /'mʌsəl/ **38**
museum /myu'ziəm/ **99**
mushrooms /'mʌʃrumz/ **61**
music /'myuzɪk/ **59**
musical instruments /,myuzɪkəl 'ɪnstrəmənts/ **96**

music store /'myuzɪk ,stɔr/ **84**
mussels /'mʌsəlz/ **65, 103**
mustache /'mʌstæʃ/ **39**
mustard /'mʌstɚd/ **64**

nail /neɪl/ **32, 37**
nail clippers /'neɪl ,klɪpɚz/ **43**
nail file /'neɪl faɪl/ **43**
nail polish /'neɪl ,palɪʃ/ **43**
nail scissors /'neɪl ,sɪzɚz/ **43**
nanny goat /'næni ,goʊt/ **101**
napkin /'næpkɪn/ **19**
napkin ring /'næpkɪn ,rɪŋ/ **19**
narrow /'næroʊ/ **52, 114**
Nashville /'næʃvɪl/ **8**
national park /,næʃənl 'park/ **99**
nature reserve /'neɪtʃɚ rɪ,zɚv/ **98**
navy blue /,neɪvi 'blu/ **53**
near /nɪr/ **114**
neat /nit/ **114**
Nebraska /nə'bræskə/ **8**
neck /nɛk/ **37**
necklace /'nɛk-lɪs/ **55**
needle /'nidl/ **47, 54**
nephew /'nɛfyu/ **11**
Neptune /'nɛptun/ **108**
nervous /'nɚvəs/ **113**
nest /nɛst/ **104**
net /nɛt/ **87, 88**
Nevada /nə'vædə/ **8**
New England /nu 'ɪŋglənd/ **8**
New Hampshire /nu 'hæmpʃɚ/ **8**
New Jersey /nu 'dʒɚzi/ **8**
New Mexico /nu 'mɛksɪkoʊ/ **8**
new moon /,nu 'mun/ **108**
New Orleans /nu 'ɔrliənz/ **8**
newscaster /'nuz,kæstɚ/ **29**
newspaper /'nuz,peɪpɚ/ **83**
newspapers /'nuz,peɪpɚz/ **60**
New Year's Eve /,nu yɪrz 'iv/ **6**
New York /nu 'yɔrk/ **8**
next to /'nɛkst tu/ **116**
nickel /'nɪkəl/ **79**
niece /nis/ **11**
nightclothes /'naɪtˀkloʊz/ **49**
nightgown /'naɪtˀgaʊn/ **49**
nightie /'naɪṭi/ **49**
nightstand /'naɪtstænd/ **17**
night table /'naɪt ,teɪbəl/ **17**
nine /naɪn/ **4**
nineteen /,naɪn'tin/ **4**
ninety /'naɪnṭi/ **4**
nipple /'nɪpəl/ **20**
no parking sign /,noʊ 'parkɪŋ ,saɪn/ **80**
no right turn sign /,noʊ raɪt 'tɚn ,saɪn/ **75**
Norfolk /'nɔrfək/ **8**
north /nɔrθ/ **8**

North Carolina /,nɔrθ kærə'laɪnə/ **8**
North Dakota /,nɔrθ də'koʊṭə/ **8**
no U-turn sign /,noʊ 'yu tɚn ,saɪn/ **75**
noodles /'nudlz/ **66**
noon /nun/ **7**
nose /noʊz/ **37**
nosebleed /'noʊzblid/ **44**
notebook /'noʊtˀbʊk/ **58**
notepad /'noʊtˀpæd/ **30**
November /noʊ'vɛmbɚ/ **6**
nozzle /'nazəl/ **72**
number pad /'nʌmbɚ ,pæd/ **85**
nurse /nɚs/ **28, 47**
nursery school /'nɚsəri ,skul/ **56**
nuts /nʌts/ **62**
nylons /'naɪlənz/

oar /ɔr/ **78, 90**
oatmeal /'oʊtˀmil/ **64, 70**
oboe /'oʊboʊ/ **96**
obstetrician /,abstə'trɪʃən/ **46**
obtuse angle /əb,tus 'æŋgəl/ **5**
ocean /'oʊʃən/ **97**
October /ak'toʊbɚ/ **6**
octopus /'aktəpəs/ **103**
Odessa /oʊ'dɛsə/ **8**
off /ɔf/ **115**
office /'ɔfɪs/ **30**
off of /'ɔf əv/ **115**
off-ramp/exit /'ɔf ræmp, 'ɛgzɪt/ **74**
Ohio /oʊ'haɪoʊ/ **8**
oil /ɔɪl/ **64**
oil tanker /'ɔɪl ,tæŋkɚ/ **78**
Oklahoma /,oʊklə'hoʊmə/ **8**
Oklahoma City /,oʊkləhoʊmə 'sɪṭi/ **8**
Omaha /'oʊmə,ha/ **8**
omelet /'amlɪt/ **70**
on /ɔn/ **115**
one /wʌn/ **4, 79**
one dollar /wʌn 'dalɚ/ **79**
one hundred /wʌn 'hʌndrɪd/ **4**
one hundred and one /wʌn ,hʌndrɪd ən 'wʌn/ **4**
one hundred percent /wʌn ,hʌndrɪd pɚ'sɛnt/ **4**
one-hundred thousand /,wʌn hʌndrɪd 'θaʊzənd/ **4**
one million /wʌn 'mɪlyən/ **4**
one thousand /wʌn 'θaʊzənd/ **4**
one-way sign /,wʌn 'weɪ ,saɪn/ **75**
onions /'ʌnyənz/ **61**
on-ramp /'ɔn ræmp/ **74**
onto /'ɔntu/ **115**
on top of /ɔn 'tap əv/ **116**
open /'oʊpən/ **41, 113**
opera /'aprə/ **93**

operation /,apə'reɪʃən/ **47**
ophthalmologist /,afθə'malədʒɪst/ **46**
opposites /'apəzɪts/ **114**
optician's /ap'tɪʃənz/ **84**
optometrist /ap'tamətrɪst/ **48**
orange /'ɔrɪndʒ/ **53, 62**
orange juice /'ɔrɪndʒ ,dʒus/ **70**
orbit /'ɔrbɪt/ **108**
orca /'ɔrkə/ **103**
orchestra pit /'ɔrkɪstrə ,pɪt/ **93**
orchid /'ɔrkɪd/ **22**
orderly /'ɔrdɚli/ **47**
Oregon /'ɔrɪgən/ **8**
orthodontist /,ɔrθə'dantɪst/ **48**
osteopath /'astiə,pæθ/ **46**
ostrich /'astrɪtʃ/ **104**
ounce /aʊns/ **68**
out box /'aʊt baks/ **30**
outdoor clothing /,aʊtdɔr 'kloʊðɪŋ/ **49**
outfield /'aʊtˀfild/ **86**
out of /'aʊt əv/ **115, 116**
outside /,aʊt'saɪd/ **116**
oval /'oʊvəl/ **5**
oven /'ʌvən/ **14**
over /'oʊvɚ/ **115**
overalls /'oʊvɚ,ɔlz/ **50**
overhead bin /,oʊvɚhɛd 'bɪn/ **77**
overhead compartment /,oʊvɚhɛd kəm'partˀmənt/ **77**
overhead projector /,oʊvɚhɛd prə'dʒɛktɚ/ **56**
overpass /'oʊvɚ,pæs/ **74**
owl /aʊl/ **104**
oxygen mask /'aksɪdʒən ,mæsk/ **77, 85**
oyster /'ɔɪstɚ/ **65**

Pacific Coast /pə,sɪfɪk 'koʊst/ **8**
Pacific Ocean /pə,sɪfɪk 'oʊʃən/ **8**
pacifier /'pæsə,faɪɚ/ **20**
package /'pækɪdʒ/ **82**
pack of envelopes /,pæk əv 'ɛnvəloʊps/ **83**
pad of paper /,pæd əv 'peɪpɚ/ **83**
paddle /'pædl/ **88, 90**
pager /'peɪdʒɚ/ **111**
pail /peɪl/ **97**
painkiller /'peɪn,kɪlɚ/ **44**
pain reliever /'peɪn rɪ,livɚ/ **44**
paint /peɪnt/ **32, 41**
paintbrush /'peɪntˀbrʌʃ/ **32, 57, 94**
paint can /'peɪntˀkæn/ **32**
painter /'peɪntɚ/ **27**
painting /'peɪntɪŋ/ **94**
paint roller /'peɪntˀroʊlɚ/ **32**

WORDLIST

paints /peɪnts/ **57**
paint tray /'peɪnt treɪ/ **32**
pajamas /pə'dʒɑməz/ **49**
pallet /'pælɪt/ **33**
palm tree /'pɑm tri/ **106**
palm /pɑm/ **37**
panties /'pæntiz/ **50**
pants /pænts/ **50, 51**
pantyhose /'pænti,houz/ **50**
papaya /pə'paɪə/ **62**
paper clip /'peɪpə ,klɪp/ **30**
paperback /'peɪpə,bæk/ **83**
parakeet /'pærə,kit/ **100**
parallel /'pærə,lɛl/ **5**
paramedic /,pærə'mɛdɪk/ **85**
parents /'pɛrənts/ **10**
park /pɑrk/ **99**
parking meter /'pɑrkɪŋ ,mɪtə/ **80**
parrot /'pærət/ **104**
part /pɑrt/ **39**
participate in a meeting /pɑr,tɪsəpeɪt ɪn ə 'mitɪŋ/ **31**
passenger /'pæsəndʒə/ **71**
passenger car /'pæsəndʒə ,kɑr/ **71**
passport /'pæsport/ **76**
pasta /'pɑstə/ **64**
patient /'peɪʃənt/ **46, 47, 48**
patio /'pæti,ou/ **22**
patio chair /'pætiou ,tʃɛr/ **22**
patio table /'pætiou ,teɪbəl/ **22**
pattern /'pætən/ **53, 54**
patterned /'pætənd/ **53**
paws /pɔz/ **100**
pay phone /'peɪ foun/ **85**
PC /,pi 'si/ **30, 109**
PDA /,pi di 'eɪ/ **111**
peach /pitʃ/ **62**
peacock /'pikɑk/ **104**
peak /pik/ **106**
peanut /'pinʌt/ **62**
peanut butter /'pinət ,bʌtə/ **63**
pear /pɛr/ **62**
pearls /pərlz/ **55**
peas /piz/ **61**
pedal /'pɛdl/ **72**
pedestrian /pə'dɛstriən/ **80**
pedestrian crossing /pə'dɛstriən ,krɔsɪŋ/ **75**
pediatrician /,pidiə'trɪʃən/ **46**
peel /pil/ **69**
peeler /'pilə/ **15**
pelican /'pɛlɪkən/ **104**
pelvis /'pɛlvɪs/ **38**
pencil /'pɛnsəl/ **30, 58, 83**
pencil holder /'pɛnsəl ,houldə/ **30**
pencil sharpener /'pɛnsəl ,ʃɑrpənə/ **58**
penguin /'pɛŋgwɪn/ **104**

Pennsylvania /,pɛnsəl'veɪnyə/ **8**
penny /'pɛni/ **79**
pepper /'pɛpə/ **64**
pepper shaker /'pɛpə ,ʃeɪkə/ **19**
percussion /pə'kʌʃən/ **96**
performing arts /pə,fɔrmɪŋ 'ɑrts/ **59**
perfume /'pəfyum/ **43**
periodical /,pɪri'ɑdɪkəl/ **83**
periodicals section /pɪri'ɑdɪkəlz ,sɛkʃən/ **60**
perm /pəm/ **42**
perpendicular /,pəpən'dɪkyələ/ **5**
personal cassette player /,pəsənəl kə'sɛt ,pleɪə/ **110**
personal check /'pəsənəl 'tʃɛk/ **79**
personal computer /,pəsənəl kəm'pyutə/ **30, 109**
pets /pɛts/ **100**
petticoat /'pɛti,kout/ **50**
pharmacist /'fɑrməsɪst/ **28**
pharmacy /'fɑrməsi/ **84**
Philadelphia /,fɪlə'dɛlfyə/ **8**
Phoenix /'finɪks/ **8**
phone /foun/ **111**
photocopier /'foutə,kɑpiə/ **30, 60**
photocopy a letter /,foutəkɑpi ə 'lɛtə/ **31**
photographer /fə'tɑgrəfə/ **29**
photography /fə'tɑgrəfi/ **94**
physical education /,fɪzɪkəl ɛdʒə'keɪʃən/ **59**
physical therapist /,fɪzɪkəl 'θɛrəpɪst/ **46**
physician /fɪ'zɪʃən/ **46**
physics /'fɪzɪks/ **59**
physiotherapist /,fɪziou'θɛrəpɪst/ **46**
piano /pi'ænou/ **96**
piccolo /'pɪkə,lou/ **96**
pickaxe /'pɪkæks/ **34**
pick up /,pɪk 'ʌp/ **41**
pick up the children /,pɪk ʌp ðə 'tʃɪldrən/ **25**
picnic table /'pɪknɪk ,teɪbəl/ **98**
picture /'pɪktʃə/ **18**
picture frame /'pɪktʃə ,freɪm/ **18**
pie /paɪ/ **66**
pier /pɪr/ **97**
Pierre /pyɛr/ **8**
pig /pɪg/ **101**
pigeon /'pɪdʒən/ **104**
piglet /'pɪglɪt/ **101**
pillow /'pɪlou/ **17**
pillowcase /'pɪlou,keɪs/ **17**
pills /pɪlz/ **44**
pilot /'paɪlət/ **77**

pin /pɪn/ **54, 55, 88**
pincushion /'pɪn,kuʃən/ **54**
pineapple /'paɪn,æpəl/ **62**
pine cone /'paɪn koun/ **106**
pine tree /'paɪn tri/ **106**
ping pong /'pɪŋ pɑŋ/ **88**
ping pong ball /'pɪŋ pɑŋ ,bɔl/ **88**
ping pong player /'pɪŋ pɑŋ ,pleɪə/ **88**
ping pong table /'pɪŋ pɑŋ ,teɪbəl/ **88**
pink /pɪŋk/ **53**
pint /paɪnt/ **68**
pipette /paɪ'pɛt/ **58**
pita bread /'pitə ,brɛd/ **65**
pitcher /'pɪtʃə/ **19, 86**
pitcher's mound /'pɪtʃəz ,maund/ **86**
pizza /'pitsə/ **66**
place mat /'pleɪs mæt/ **19**
plaid /plæd/ **53**
plane /pleɪn/ **32**
planets /'plænɪts/ **108**
plant /plænt/ **18**
planter /'plæntə/ **18, 23**
plant flowers /,plænt 'flauəz/ **23**
plastic wrap /'plæstɪk ,ræp/ **64**
plate /pleɪt/ **19**
platform /'plæt,fɔrm/ **71**
playing music /,pleɪ-ɪŋ 'myuzɪk/ **94**
pliers /'plaɪəz/ **32**
plug /plʌg/ **21**
plum /plʌm/ **62**
plumber /'plʌmə/ **27**
plus /plʌs/ **4**
Pluto /'plutou/ **108**
pocket /'pɑkɪt/ **52**
pocket calculator /,pɑkɪt 'kælkyə,leɪtə/ **111**
point /pɔɪnt/ **40**
polar bear /'poulə ,bɛr/ **102**
Polaroid™ camera /,poulərɔɪd 'kæmrə/ **111**
pole /poul/ **91**
police car /pə'lis ,kɑr/ **85**
police officer /pə'lis ,ɔfəsə/ **28, 36, 85**
police station /pə'lis ,steɪʃən/ **85**
polka-dotted /'poukə ,dɑtɪd/ **53**
polyester /'pɑli,ɛstə/ **54**
pond /pɑnd/ **106**
pony tail /'pouni ,teɪl/ **39**
pork /pɔrk/ **65**
pork chops /'pɔrk tʃɑps/ **65**
porter /'pɔrtə/ **76**
Portland /'pɔrtlənd/ **8**
postal clerk /'poustl ,klərk/ **82**
postcard /'poustkard/ **82**

poster /'poustə/ **56**
postmark /'poustmark/ **82**
pot /'pɑt/ **15**
pot holder /'pɑt ,houldə/ **15**
pot roast /'pɑt roust/ **65**
potato chips /pə'teɪtə ,tʃɪps/ **67, 83**
potatoes /pə'teɪtouz/ **61**
potato salad /pə,teɪtou 'sæləd/ **65**
potter's wheel /'pɑtəz ,wil/ **94**
pottery /'pɑtəri/ **94**
potty chair /'pɑti ,tʃɛr/ **20**
pouch /pautʃ/ **102**
pound /paund/ **68**
pour /pɔr/ **41, 69**
power drill /'pauə ,drɪl/ **32**
power saw /'pauə ,sɔ/ **32**
pre-school /'priskul/ **56**
prescription /prɪ'skrɪpʃən/ **46**
press /prɛs/ **41**
print a copy /,prɪnt ə 'kɑpi/ **31**
printer /'prɪntə/ **109**
prison /'prɪzən/ **36**
prison officer /'prɪzən ,ɔfəsə/ **36**
professor /prə'fɛsə/ **28**
promenade /,prɑmə'neɪd/ **97**
prosecuting attorney /'prɑsə,kyutɪŋ ə'təni/ **36**
prosecutor /'prɑsə,kyutə/ **36**
protractor /prou'træktə/ **58**
prune /prun/ **62**
pull /pul/ **40**
pumpkin /'pʌmpkɪn/ **61**
pumps /pʌmps/ **49**
pupil /'pyupəl/ **38**
puppy /'pʌpi/ **100**
purple /'pəpəl/ **53**
purse /pəs/ **55**
push /puʃ/ **40**
put down /,put 'daun/ **41**
put on make-up /,put ɔn 'meɪkʌp/ **12**

quart /kwɔrt/ **68**
quarter /'kwɔrtə/ **79**
quarter full /,kwɔrtə 'ful/ **68**
quilt /kwɪlt/ **17**
quilting /'kwɪltɪŋ/ **94**

rabbit /'ræbɪt/ **100, 101**
raccoon /ræ'kun/ **102**
racehorse /'reɪshɔrs/ **87**
radio /'reɪdi,ou/ **73, 110**
radius /'reɪdiəs/ **5**
railroad crossing /'reɪlroud ,krɔsɪŋ/ **75**
railroad crossing sign /'reɪlroud ,krɔsɪŋ ,saɪn/ **75**
railroad station /'reɪlroud ,steɪʃən/ **71**

stuffed animal /ˌstʌft ˈænəməl/ **20**

stuffed peppers /ˌstʌft ˈpɛpəz/ **66**

style /staɪl/ **42**

styling brush /ˈstaɪlɪŋ ˌbrʌʃ/ **42**

submarine sandwich /ˌsʌbmərin ˈsændwɪtʃ/ **67**

subway entrance /ˈsʌbweɪ ˌɛntrəns/ **81**

subway station /ˈsʌbweɪ ˌsteɪʃən/ **71**

sugar /ˈʃʊgə/ **64**

suit /sut/ **50, 51**

suitcase /ˈsutˑkeɪs/ **35, 76**

summer /ˈsʌmə/ **107**

Sun /sʌn/ **108**

sunbather /ˈsʌnˌbeɪðə/ **97**

sunburn /ˈsʌnbən/ **45**

Sunday /ˈsʌndi/ **6**

sunglasses /ˈsʌnˌglæsɪz/ **97**

sunny /ˈsʌni/ **107**

sunscreen /ˈsʌnskrin/ **97**

suntan lotion /ˈsʌntæn ˌloʊʃən/ **97**

supermarket /ˈsupəˌmarkɪt/ **63**

supermarket counters /ˈsupəmarkɪt ˌkaʊntəz/ **65**

surfboard /ˈsəfbɔrd/ **90, 97**

surfer /ˈsəfə/ **90, 97**

surfing /ˈsəfɪŋ/ **90**

surgeon /ˈsədʒən/ **47**

surgery /ˈsədʒəri/ **47**

surgical collar /ˌsədʒɪkəl ˈkalə/ **47**

surgical gloves /ˌsədʒɪkəl ˈglʌvz/ **47**

surprised /səˈpraɪzd/ **113**

suspect /ˈsʌspɛkt/ **36**

suspenders /səˈspɛndəz/ **55**

suspicious /səˈspɪʃəs/ **113**

SUV /ˌɛs yu ˈvi/ **72**

swallow /ˈswaloʊ/ **104**

swamp /swamp/ **106**

swan /swan/ **104**

sweater /ˈswɛtə/ **49**

sweatshirt /ˈswɛt-ʃət/ **50, 51**

sweep the floor /ˌswip ðə ˈflɔr/ **25**

swimmer /ˈswimə/ **90**

swimming cap /ˈswimɪŋ ˌkæp/ **90**

swimming pool /ˈswimɪŋ ˌpul/ **90**

swimming trunks /ˈswimɪŋ ˈtrʌŋks/ **51, 97**

swimming /ˈswimɪŋ/ **90**

swimsuit /ˈswimsut/ **51, 97**

swings /swɪŋz/ **57**

Swiss cheese /ˌswɪs ˈtʃiz/ **65**

symphony orchestra /ˌsɪmfəni ˈɔrkɪstrə/ **93**

syringe /səˈrɪndʒ/ **47**

table tennis /ˈteɪbəl ˌtɛnɪs/ **88**

tablespoon /ˈteɪbəlˌspun/ **19, 68**

tablets /ˈtæblɪts/ **44**

tackle /ˈtækəl/ **86**

taco /ˈtakoʊ/ **67**

tail /teɪl/ **77, 100, 103, 104**

tailor /ˈteɪlə/ **54**

take /teɪk/ **41**

take a bath /ˌteɪk ə ˈbæθ/ **12**

take a shower /ˌteɪk ə ˈʃaʊə/ **12**

takeoff /ˈteɪkɔf/ **77**

take the bus to school /ˌteɪk ðə ˈbʌs tə ˌskul/ **25**

take the children to school /ˌteɪk ðə ˌtʃɪldrən tə ˈskul/ **25**

talk /tɔk/ **40**

tall /tɔl/ **39**

Tallahassee /ˌtæləˈhæsi/ **8**

Tampa /ˈtæmpə/ **8**

tangerine /ˌtændʒəˈrin/ **62**

tape /teɪp/ **30, 110**

tape deck /ˈteɪp dɛk/ **110**

tape measure /ˈteɪp ˌmɛʒə/ **32, 54**

taxi /ˈtæksi/ **71**

taxi driver /ˈtæksi ˌdraɪvə/ **71**

tea /ti/ **64, 66, 70**

tea kettle /ˈti ˌkɛtl/ **15**

teacher /ˈtitʃə/ **28, 56**

teapot /ˈtipat/ **19**

tear /tɛr/ **41, 54**

teaspoon /ˈtispun/ **19, 68**

technical school /ˈtɛknɪkəl ˌskul/ **56**

teddy bear /ˈtɛdi ˌbɛr/ **20**

tee /ti/ **89**

teenager /ˈtiˌneɪdʒə/ **9**

teeter-totter /ˈtitə ˌtatə/ **57**

teeth /tiθ/ **38**

telecommunications /ˌtɛləkəmyunəˈkeɪʃənz/ **110**

telemarketer /ˈtɛləˌmarkɪtə/ **29**

telephone /ˈtɛləˌfoʊn/ **30, 111**

telescope /ˈtɛləˌskoʊp/ **94**

television /ˈtɛləˌvɪʒən/ **56, 110**

temperature /ˈtɛmprətʃə/ **44, 107**

temple /ˈtɛmpəl/ **38**

ten /tɛn/ **4**

Tennessee /ˌtɛnəˈsi/ **8**

ten percent /ˌtɛn pəˈsɛnt/ **4**

ten thousand /tɛn ˈθaʊzənd/ **4**

tennis /ˈtɛnɪs/ **88**

tennis ball /ˈtɛnɪs ˌbɔl/ **88**

tennis player /ˈtɛnɪs ˈpleɪə/ **88**

tennis racket /ˈtɛnɪs ˌrækɪt/ **88**

tent /tɛnt/ **98**

tentacle /ˈtɛntəkəl/ **103**

terminal /ˈtəmənəl/ **60, 76**

test tube /ˈtɛst tub/ **58**

textbook /ˈtɛkstbʊk/ **56**

Thanksgiving Day /ˌθæŋksˈgɪvɪŋ ˌdeɪ/ **6**

theater /ˈθiətə/ **93**

therapist /ˈθɛrəpɪst/ **46**

thermometer /θəˈmamətə/ **44**

thick /θɪk/ **114**

thigh /θaɪ/ **37**

thimble /ˈθɪmbəl/ **54**

thin /θɪn/ **39, 114**

third /θəd/ **4**

third full /ˌθəd ˈfʊl/ **68**

thirteen /ˌθəˈtin/ **4**

thirty /ˈθəti/ **4**

thread /θrɛd/ **54**

three /θri/ **4**

three quarters full /ˌθri kwɔrtəz ˈfʊl/ **68**

throat /θroʊt/ **38**

throat lozenges /ˈθroʊt ˌlazəndʒɪz/ **44**

through /θru/ **116**

throw /θroʊ/ **92**

throw pillow /ˈθroʊ ˌpɪloʊ/ **18**

thumb /θʌm/ **37**

thumbtacks /ˈθʌm tæks/ **83**

Thursday /ˈθəzdi/ **6**

ticket /ˈtɪkɪt/ **71, 76**

tie /taɪ/ **51**

tie clip /ˈtaɪ klɪp/ **55**

tiger /ˈtaɪgə/ **102**

tight /taɪt/ **2, 114**

tights /taɪts/ **50**

tile /taɪl/ **16**

time /taɪm/ **7**

time cards /ˈtaɪm kardz/ **33**

time clock /ˈtaɪm klak/ **33**

times /taɪmz/ **4**

timetable /ˈtaɪmˌteɪbəl/ **71**

tire /taɪə/ **73**

tissues /ˈtɪʃuz/ **44**

title /ˈtaɪtl/ **60**

to /tu/ **115**

toast /toʊst/ **70**

toaster /ˈtoʊstə/ **15**

toddler /ˈtadlə/ **9**

toe /toʊ/ **37**

toilet /ˈtɔɪlɪt/ **16**

toilet paper /ˈtɔɪlɪtˑ ˌpeɪpə/ **16**

toiletries /ˈtɔɪlətriz/ **43**

toll booth /ˈtoʊl buθ/ **74**

toll booth attendant /ˈtoʊl buθ əˌtɛndənt/ **74**

tomatoes /təˈmeɪtoʊz/ **61, 63**

tongs /taŋz/ **58**

tongue /tʌŋ/ **38**

toolbar /ˈtulbar/ **109**

tool belt /ˈtul bɛlt/ **34**

toolbox /ˈtulbaks/ **32**

tools /tulz/ **32**

tooth /tuθ/ **38, 48**

toothache /ˈtuθeɪk/ **44**

toothbrush /ˈtuθbrʌʃ/ **16**

toothbrush holder /ˈtuθbrʌʃ ˌhoʊldə/ **16**

toothpaste /ˈtuθpeɪst/ **16**

top /tap/ **5**

topaz /ˈtoʊpæz/ **55**

tortoise /ˈtɔrtəs/ **102**

tote bag /ˈtoʊtˑ bæg/ **55**

touch /tʌtʃ/ **40**

tour guide /ˈtʊr gaɪd/ **99**

tourist /ˈtʊrɪst/ **99**

towards /tɔrdz/ **116**

towel dry /ˌtaʊəl ˈdraɪ/ **42**

towel rack /ˈtaʊəl ˌræk/ **16**

towel /ˈtaʊəl/ **42**

townhouse /ˈtaʊnhaʊs/ **13**

towrope /ˈtoʊroʊp/ **90**

tow truck /ˈtoʊ trʌk/ **85**

toys /tɔɪz/ **57**

toy store /ˈtɔɪ stɔr/ **84**

track /træk/ **71**

traffic /ˈtræfɪk/ **80**

traffic light /ˈtræfɪk ˌlaɪt/ **74, 80**

trail /treɪl/ **91, 98**

trailer /ˈtreɪlə/ **72**

train /treɪn/ **71**

train station /ˈtreɪn ˌsteɪʃən/ **71**

train track /ˈtreɪn træk/ **75**

trash bags /ˈtræʃ bægz/ **64**

trash can /ˈtræʃ kæn/ **14, 81**

travel agent /ˈtrævəl ˌeɪdʒənt/ **29**

traveler's check /ˈtrævləz ˌtʃɛk/ **79**

tray /treɪ/ **58, 77**

treadmill /ˈtrɛdmɪl/ **92**

tree /tri/ **22, 106**

triangle /ˈtraɪˌæŋgəl/ **58**

tricycle /ˈtraɪsɪkəl/ **57**

tripod /ˈtraɪpad/ **111**

trombone /tramˈboʊn/ **96**

tropical fish /ˌtrapɪkəl ˈfɪʃ/ **100**

trout /traʊt/ **103**

trowel /ˈtraʊəl/ **23, 34**

truck /trʌk/ **72**

truck driver /ˈtrʌk ˌdraɪvə/ **27**

trumpet /ˈtrʌmpɪt/ **96**

trunk /trʌŋk/ **73, 102**

T-shirt /ˈti ʃət/ **50, 51**

tub /tʌb/ **68**

tuba /ˈtubə/ **96**

tube /tub/ **68**

Tucson /ˈtusan/ **8**

Tuesday /ˈtuzdi/ **6**

tulip /'tulɪp/ **22**
tumble dryer /ˌtʌmbəl 'draɪɚ/ **21**
tuna fish /'tunə ˌfɪʃ/ **63**
tuner /'tunɚ/ **110**
turkey /'tɚki/ **101**
turn signal /'tɚn ˌsɪgnəl/ **73**
turnstile /'tɚnstaɪl/ **71**
turquoise /'tɚkwɔɪz/ **53**
turtleneck /'tɚtlˌnɛk/ **49**
tusk /tʌsk/ **102, 103**
tuxedo /tʌk'sidoʊ/ **51**
TV /ˌti 'vi/ **110**
TV antenna /ˌti vi æn'tɛnə/ **13**
TV screen /ˌti 'vi ˌskrin/ **110**
tweezers /'twizɚz/ **43**
twelve /twɛlv/ **4**
twelve o'clock /ˌtwɛlv ə'klɑk/ **7**
twenty percent /ˌtwɛnti pɚ'sɛnt/ **4**
twenty /ˌtwɛnti/ **4**
twenty-one /ˌtwɛnti 'wʌn/ **4**
twin bed /ˌtwɪn 'bɛd/ **17**
two /tu/ **4**
two-wheeled vehicles /ˌtu wild 'viɪkəl/ **72**

umbrella /ʌm'brɛlə/ **22, 49**
umpire /'ʌmpaɪɚ/ **86**
uncle /'ʌŋkəl/ **11**
under /'ʌndɚ/ **115, 116**
underneath /ˌʌndɚ'niθ/ **116**
undershirt /'ʌndɚˌʃɚt/ **51**
underwear /'ʌndɚˌwɛr/ **50, 51**
United States /yuˌnaɪtɪd 'steɪts/ **8**
university /ˌyunə'vɚsəti/ **56**
up /ʌp/ **115**
upper arm /ˌʌpɚ 'ɑrm/ **37**
Uranus /yʊ'reɪnəs/ **108**
Utah /'yutɑ/ **8**

vacuum cleaner /'vækyum ˌklinɚ/ **21**
vacuum the house /ˌvækyum ðə 'haʊs/ **25**
Valentine's Day /'væləntaɪnz ˌdeɪ/ **6**
valley /'væli/ **106**
van /væn/ **72, 98**
vase /veɪz/ **18**
VCR /ˌvi si 'ɑr/ **110**
vegetable garden /'vɛdʒtəbəl ˌgɑrdn/ **22**
vegetables /'vɛdʒtəbəlz/ **66**
vehicle /'viɪkəl/ **72**
vein /veɪn/ **38**
Velcro™ /'vɛlkroʊ/ **54**
vendor /'vɛndɚ/ **81**
Venus /'vinəs/ **108**
Vermont /vɚ'mɑnt/ **8**

vest /vɛst/ **51**
veterinarian /ˌvɛtərə'nɛriən/ **28**
video camera /'vɪdioʊ ˌkæmrə/ **111**
video cassette /'vɪdioʊ kəˌsɛt/ **110**
video cassette recorder /ˌvɪdioʊ kəˌsɛt rɪ'kɔrdɚ/ **56, 110**
video games /'vɪdioʊ ˌgeɪmz/ **95, 110**
video store /'vɪdioʊ ˌstɔr/ **84**
vinegar /'vɪnɪgɚ/ **64**
viola /vi'oʊlə/ **96**
violin /ˌvaɪə'lɪn/ **96**
Virginia /vɚ'dʒɪnyə/ **8**
vise /vaɪs/ **32**
V-neck sweater /ˌvi nɛk 'swɛtɚ/ **49**
vocalist /'voʊkəlɪst/ **93**
vocational school /voʊ'keɪʃənl ˌskul/ **56**
volleyball /'vɑliˌbɔl/ **87**
volleyball player /'vɑlibɔl ˌpleɪɚ/ **87**

waist /weɪst/ **37**
waistband /'weɪstbænd/ **52**
waiter /'weɪtɚ/ **27, 66**
waiting room /'weɪtɪŋ ˌrum/ **47**
waitress /'weɪtrɪs/ **27**
wake up /ˌweɪk 'ʌp/ **12**
walk /wɔk/ **92**
walkie-talkie /ˌwɔki 'tɔki/ **34**
Walkman™ /'wɔkmən/ **110**
walk sign /'wɔk saɪn/ **80**
walk the dog /ˌwɔk ðə 'dɔg/ **25**
walkway /'wɔk-weɪ/ **13**
wall /wɔl/ **24**
wall unit /'wɔl ˌyunɪt/ **18**
wallet /'wɑlɪt/ **55**
wallpaper /'wɔlˌpeɪpɚ/ **17**
walnut /'wɔlnʌt/ **62**
walrus /'wɔlrəs/ **103**
warehouse /'wɛrhaʊs/ **33**
warm /wɔrm/ **107**
warm-up suit /'wɔrm ʌp ˌsut/ **51**
wash /wɑʃ/ **42, 69**
wash cloth /'wɑʃ klɔθ/ **16**
washing machine /'wɑʃɪŋ məˌʃin/ **21**
Washington /'wɑʃɪŋtən/ **8**
Washington D.C. /'wɑʃɪŋtən ˌdi 'si/ **8**
wash the dishes /ˌwɑʃ ðə 'dɪʃɪz/ **25**
wash your face /wɑʃ yɚ 'feɪs/ **12**
wasp /wɑsp/ **105**
wastepaper basket /'weɪstpeɪpɚ ˌbæskɪt/ **30**

watch /wɑtʃ/ **7, 55**
watch TV /wɑtʃ ˌti vi/ **12**
water buffalo /'wɔtɚ ˌbʌfəloʊ/ **102**
watercress /'wɔtɚˌkrɛs/ **61**
waterfall /'wɔtɚˌfɔl/ **106**
watering can /'wɔtɚɪŋ ˌkæn/ **23**
watermelon /'wɔtɚˌmɛlən/ **62**
water ski /'wɔtɚ ˌski/ **90**
water-skier /'wɔtɚ ˌskiɚ/ **90**
water skiing /'wɔtɚ ˌski-ɪŋ/ **90**
water sports /'wɔtɚ ˌsports/ **90**
water the plants /ˌwɔtɚ ðə 'plænts/ **23**
wave /weɪv/ **40, 97**
wavy hair /ˌweɪvi 'hɛr/ **39**
weather /'wɛðɚ/ **107**
Wednesday /'wɛnzdi/ **6**
weigh /weɪ/ **69**
weights /weɪts/ **92**
west /wɛst/ **8**
West Coast /ˌwɛst 'koʊst/ **8**
West Virginia /ˌwɛst vɚ'dʒɪnyə/ **8**
wet /wɛt/ **114**
wheel /wil/ **72**
wheelbarrow /'wilˌbæroʊ/ **23, 34**
wheelchair /'wil-tʃɛr/ **47**
whipped cream /ˌwɪpt 'krim/ **66**
whisk /wɪsk/ **15**
whiskers /'wɪskɚz/ **100**
white /waɪt/ **53**
whiteboard /'waɪtˌbɔrd/ **56**
whiteboard marker /'waɪtˌbɔrd ˌmɑrkɚ/ **56**
white bread /ˌwaɪt 'brɛd/ **65**
white out™ /'waɪt aʊt/ **30, 83**
white wine /ˌwaɪt 'waɪn/ **64, 66**
whole trout /ˌhoʊl 'traʊt/ **65**
whole wheat bread /ˌhoʊl 'wit ˌbrɛd/ **65**
wide /waɪd/ **52, 114**
widow /'wɪdoʊ/ **9**
widower /'wɪdoʊɚ/ **9**
width /wɪdθ/ **5**
wife /waɪf/ **10**
window cleaner /'wɪndoʊ ˌklinɚ/ **27, 64**
window frame /'wɪndoʊ ˌfreɪm/ **24**
window pane /'wɪndoʊ ˌpeɪn/ **24**
window seat /'wɪndoʊ ˌsit/ **77**
window /'wɪndoʊ/ **13, 18, 24, 77, 109**
windshield /'wɪndʃild/ **73**
windshield wiper /'wɪndʃild ˌwaɪpɚ/ **73**

windsurfer /'wɪndˌsɚfɚ/ **90**
windsurfing /'wɪndˌsɚfɪŋ/ **90**
windy /'wɪndi/ **107**
wine glass /'waɪn glæs/ **19**
wine list /'waɪn lɪst/ **66**
wing /wɪŋ/ **77, 104**
winter /'wɪntɚ/ **107**
winter sports /ˌwɪntɚ 'sports/ **91**
Wisconsin /wɪs'kɑnsɪn/ **8**
withdrawal slip /wɪθ'drɔəl ˌslɪp/ **79**
witness /'wɪtˌnɪs/ **36**
wok /wɑk/ **15**
wolf /wʊlf/ **102**
woman /'wʊmən/ **9**
women's wear /'wɪmɪnz ˌwɛr/ **49**
woodchuck /'wʊdtʃʌk/ **105**
woods /wʊdz/ **106**
woodwinds /'wʊdwɪndz/ **96**
woodworking /'wʊdˌwɚkɪŋ/ **94**
wool /wʊl/ **54**
workbench /'wɚkbɛntʃ/ **32**
worker /'wɚkɚ/ **33**
work on a computer /ˌwɚk ɔn ə kəm'pyutɚ/ **31**
work station /'wɚk ˌsteɪʃən/ **33**
wrapping paper /'ræpɪŋ ˌpeɪpɚ/ **83**
wrench /rɛntʃ/ **32**
wrestler /'rɛslɚ/ **88**
wrestling /'rɛslɪŋ/ **88**
wrist /rɪst/ **37**
write /raɪt/ **41**
Wyoming /waɪ'oʊmɪŋ/ **8**

X-ray /'ɛks reɪ/ **46**
X-ray machine /'ɛks reɪ məˌʃin/ **76**
xylophone /'zaɪləˌfoʊn/ **96**

yacht /yɑt/ **78**
yard line /'yɑrd laɪn/ **86**
yarn /yɑrn/ **54**
yellow /'yɛloʊ/ **53**
yellow light /ˌyɛloʊ 'laɪt/ **74**
yield sign /'yild saɪn/ **75**
yogurt /'yoʊgɚt/ **63**

zebra /'zibrə/ **102**
zero percent /ˌzɪroʊ pɚ'sɛnt/ **4**
zip code /'zɪp koʊd/ **82**
zipper /'zɪpɚ/ **52**
zoo /zu/ **99**
zucchini /zu'kini/ **61**

1 NUMBERS, TIME, HOLIDAYS

1.1   Write these words out in the correct order

third   fifth   first   fourth   second

1. _____   2. _____   3. _____   4. _____   5. _____

1.2   What shapes are these objects? Put them in the correct column.

dice	calculator	tire	plate	egg
watermelon	baseball	door	clock	flag

Oval   **Circle**   **Rectangle**

_____   _____   _____

_____   _____   _____

                     _____   _____

                     _____   _____

1.3   When do these holidays happen? Draw a line from the holiday to its month.

Father's Day	November
Thanksgiving	May
Valentine's Day	July
Christmas Day	June
Memorial Day	October
Halloween	December
Independence Day	February

1.4   Circle the time you would do the activity.

1. Eat breakfast	7:30 a.m.	7:30 p.m.
2. Go to the store	2:00 a.m.	2:00 p.m.
3. Mow the lawn	4:00 a.m.	4:00 p.m.
4. Eat lunch	noon	midnight
5. Go to sleep	11 o'clock in the morning	11 o'clock in the evening

EXERCISES

1.1 **What do you do in the morning? Put the verbs in order.**

get up	dry yourself	1. _____	4. _____
take a shower	get dressed	2. _____	5. _____
wake up	go to work	3. _____	6. _____

2.2 **Use the information about Michael Douglas to complete the application form.**

Michael Douglas	09/25/1944	994-9872
1106 Hollywood Drive, Los Angeles, CA	Actor	Male
98554	Married	American
Catherine Zeta-Jones	2 children	New Brunswick, New Jersey

1. First name _____
2. Last name _____
3. Sex _____
4. Occupation _____
5. Address _____
6. Zip code _____
7. Telephone number _____

8. Nationality _____
9. Date of birth _____
10. Place of birth _____
11. Marital status _____
12. Husband's/wife's name _____
13. Number of children _____

2.3 **Put the male and female equivalents in the correct column.**

granddaughter, sister, nephew, half-sister, father, aunt, grandmother, mother-in-law, stepfather, stepson

	Male	Female		Male	Female
Example	widower	widow			
1.	brother	_____	6.	_____	stepdaughter
2.	_____	mother	7.	father-in-law	_____
3.	uncle	_____	8.	half-brother	_____
4.	grandfather	_____	9.	grandson	_____
5.	_____	niece	10.	stepmother	_____

2.4 **Marital status. Write these words out correctly.**

1. insleg _____
2. riedram _____
3. idwwo _____

4. mrreiedar _____
5. vdecroid _____

3 HOUSING

3.1   Where in your house are these objects? Draw a line to link the objects to the correct rooms.

toilet		dresser
oven	kitchen	coffee table
laundry basket	bathroom	sofa/couch
armchair	dining room	dining table
headboard	living room	napkin
quilt	bedroom	spice rack
microwave		

3.2   Choose the part of the house where we normally do these things.

dining room, bedroom (2), bathroom (2), kitchen (2), yard (2)

Example   We usually watch the television in the <u>living room</u>.

1. We usually sleep in the   _____
2. We eat our meals in the   _____
3. We wash our hair in the   _____
4. We cook a barbecue in the   _____
5. We brush our teeth in the   _____

6. We make dinner in the   _____
7. We sit in the sun in the   _____
8. We wash the dishes in the   _____
9. We make the beds in the   _____

3.3 Write the name of the part of the house where you would find these items and cross out the object that is in the wrong place.

oven	closet	toilet	armchair	lawn
freezer	dressing table	toothbrush	razor	shed
dishwasher	alarm clock	tile	magazine rack	bush
sink	bath tub	mirror	sofa	swing
fridge	lamp	quilt	bookcase	crib
~~swing~~	mattress	sink	coffee table	fence
				hedge

Example kitchen   1. _____   2. _____   3. _____   4. _____

3.4   Complete the words. All these things go on the dining room table.

1. f_rk
2. sp_on
3. w_ne glas_
4. plat_
5. nap_in

6. kn_fe
7. t_bl_spoo_
8. s_lt
9. p_pper
10. t_asp_on

EXERCISES

4 WORK

4.1 Match the place of work to the job.

hospital, court, studio, restaurant, school, university, kitchen, office, bank

1. secretary _____

2. nurse _____

3. teacher _____

4. professor _____

5. judge _____

6. photographer _____

7. bank teller _____

8. cook _____

9. waiter _____

4.2 Fill in the verbs to complete the word. All of the verbs are activities in the office.

		O					a meeting

	F			papers

send a	F		

		I				a letter

				C				a letter

	E			an e-mail

4.3 Match the pictures and the words. Put the correct number next to the word.

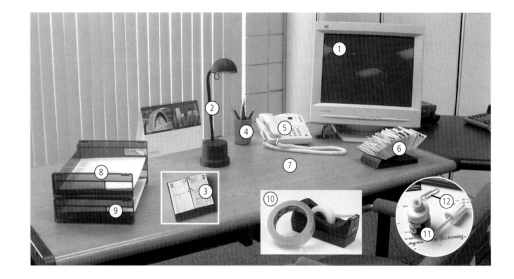

pencil holder ☐ white out™ ☐ telephone ☐ ☐

in box ☐ Rolodex ☐ lamp ☐ ☐

paper clip ☐ PC ☐ desk calendar ☐ ☐

out box ☐ tape ☐ desk ☐ ☐

5 THE BODY

5.1 Fill in the blanks to complete the physical description.
Each dash represents a letter.

This man has _ _ _ _ _   _ _ _ _ _ hair. He has _ _ _ eyes and a _ _ _ _ nose.

He has _ _ _ _ eyelashes and thick _ _ _ _ _ _ _ _ . His mouth is _ _ _ _ _ and

his _ _ _ _ are small too. He has a _ _ _ _ beard and a _ _ _ _ _ _ _ _ .

5.2 Write the verbs of movement under the correct picture.

to frown, to cry, to push, to pull, to sit, to talk, to sing, to hug, to shake hands, to wave

1. _____   2. _____   3. _____   4. _____   5. _____

6. _____   7. _____   8. _____   9. _____   10. _____

5.3 Match the opposites. Draw a line to connect them.

1. tall   **2.** dark hair   **3.** heavy   **4.** straight hair   **5.** short hair

a) thin   **b)** long hair   **c)** short   **d)** blond hair   **e)** curly hair

5.4 Put these words in the correct box according to where they are on our bodies.

thigh, nose, wrist, hip, waist, palm, ankle, calf, knee, elbow, stomach, ears, forehead, kneecap, cheek, fingers, thumb, back, mouth, lips

Head/Face	Arm/Hand	Leg	Body
_____	_____	_____	_____
_____	_____	_____	_____
_____	_____	_____	_____
_____	_____		
_____	_____		
_____			

EXERCISES

6 FOOD

6.1 Complete the restaurant dialogue with the words below.

apple pie, shrimp cocktail, roast beef, baked potato, bottled water

WAITER   Hello, sir. What would you like to eat?

CUSTOMER   For an appetizer I would like _____.

WAITER   And for the main course?

CUSTOMER   I would like _____ and
           a _____ .

WAITER   Would you like dessert?

CUSTOMER   Yes. Can I have _____ please?

WAITER   And to drink?

CUSTOMER   I would like _____ .

6.2 Put these words in the correct boxes.

chicken, orange juice, pepper, oil, bacon, ground beef, pork chops, sugar, cereal, vinegar, shrimp, liver, salt, pasta, rice, lobster, crab, cookies, beer, mineral water

Meat	Drinks	Fish and seafood	Dry goods and condiments	
____	____	____	____	____
____	____	____	____	____
____	____	____	____	____
____			____	____
____			____	

6.3 Food word soup

Look at these pictures. Find the words for these foods in the word soup.

D	O	U	G	H	N	U	T	G	E	W	O
I	Y	S	M	Q	H	N	A	B	N	D	W
S	S	O	U	P	M	U	C	T	A	U	N
E	O	G	L	I	O	C	O	H	P	R	K
C	R	D	P	Z	C	K	W	P	I	C	M
R	A	V	A	Z	T	B	O	V	K	P	G
E	D	F	N	A	K	E	A	M	J	E	S
A	Q	S	U	R	N	A	P	K	I	N	E
M	H	A	M	B	U	R	G	E	R	T	R

7 TRANSPORTATION

7.1 Use the words in the box to finish the sentences below.

engine, train station, passenger, platform, track, luggage compartment, bus stop, timetable

1. You should never walk on the _____

2. You wait for the train on the _____

3. You can leave your bags in a _____

4. You wait for a bus at the _____

5. To know what time the train leaves, look at the _____

6. When you ride on a train, you are a _____

7. The car that pulls the train is the _____

8. The train arrives in the _____

7.2 Number the words.

roof rack ☐   bumper ☐   hood ☐   trunk ☐   exhaust pipe ☐

side mirror ☐   headlight ☐   gas cap ☐   tire ☐   door ☐

7.3 Find the missing letters to make a new word.

Word	Missing letter	Word	Missing letter	Word	Missing letter
1. –icket	t	4. custo–s		7. p–ssport	
2. b–llhop		5. su–tcase		8. –uggage cart	
3. baggage claim a–ea		6. boardi–g pass		New word _ _ _ _ _ _ _ _ _ _ _ _ _ _	

7.4 Put these vehicles in the correct category.

sedan, yacht, hatchback, cabin cruiser, rowboat, four-wheel drive, helicopter, convertible, oil tanker, cruise ship, station wagon, ferry, jet plane

Air	Land	Sea

EXERCISES

8 COMMUNITY

8.1 Put the words in the correct boxes.

coin slot, fire hydrant, stretcher, drip, ladder, hose, smoke, phonecard, ambulance, receiver, oxygen mask, fire extinguisher, paramedic

Fire station	Ambulance service	Phone booth

8.2 Draw a line to connect the place with what you can buy there.

1.	optician's	a)	stamp
2.	pharmacy	b)	radio
3.	candystore	c)	medicine
4.	sports store	d)	sunglasses
5.	music store	e)	tennis racket
6.	electronics store	f)	CD or cassette tape
7.	post office	g)	chocolate bar

8.3 Label the following items in the boxes provided.

letter, address, envelope,
postmark, zip code,
postcard, stamp

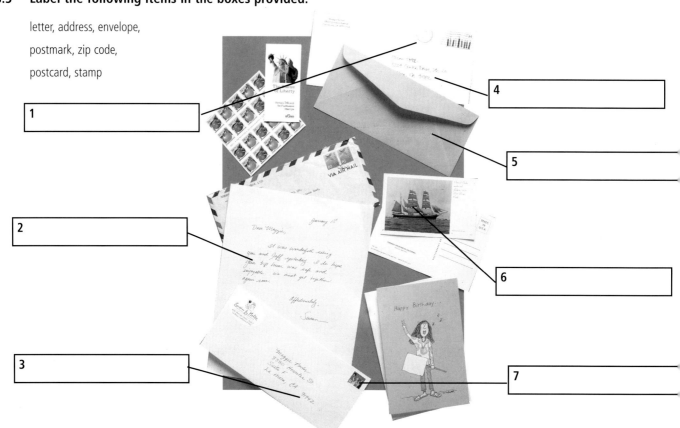

1

4

5

2

6

3

7

9 SPORTS

9.1 **Match the words to their sports type.**

speed skating   basketball

surfing   [water sports]   baseball

sailing   [individual sports]   downhill skiing

golf   [winter sports]   rowing

tennis   [team sports]   figure skating

football   diving

9.2 **Baseball word soup. Find 8 words connected with baseball.**

J	S	C	M	O	Z	P	A	C	H
D	T	N	A	F	M	I	T	T	D
B	A	S	E	T	W	T	B	Q	I
O	D	T	P	E	C	C	I	G	N
T	I	O	L	V	M	H	B	Y	F
G	U	M	P	I	R	E	E	R	I
N	M	C	L	S	A	R	Y	R	E
K	X	H	J	D	K	U	F	J	L
E	I	O	U	T	F	I	E	L	D

9.3 **Answer these questions about sports equipment.**

1.	Do football players wear boxing trunks?	No, they don't.
2.	Do wrestlers wear snorkels?	
3.	Do boxers wear trunks?	
4.	Do bowlers wear mitts?	
5.	Do volleyball players wear goggles?	
6.	Do boxers wear goggles?	
7.	Do cyclists wear helmets?	
8.	Do roller-skaters wear helmets?	
9.	Do swimmers wear gloves?	
10.	Do scuba divers wear shoulder pads?	

EXERCISES

10 ENTERTAINMENT

10.1 Match each hobby to one piece of equipment.

photography | knitting needles | | telescope | painting

knitting | potter's wheel | | binoculars | astronomy

pottery | brush | | camera | bird-watching

10.2 Put the words in the correct box.

pier   swimsuit

surfboard   cooler

float   seashell

beach towel wave

sea   shovel

bucket   sunglasses

Things you take to the beach	Things you find at the beach

10.3 Find the missing letters to make a new word.

Word	Missing letter	Word	Missing letter	Word	Missing letter
1. ba–kpack	c	**4.** sign–ost		**7.** sleepin– bag	
2. p–th		**5.** camps–te			
3. fisher–an		**6.** hiki–g		**New word** _ _ _ _ _ _ _ _ _	

10.4 What games are these? Unscramble the letters.

1. sches _____

2. ecid _____

3. omteucpr_____ games

4. nomamgkacb _____

5. kcreshce_____

6. rdsca _____

10.5 Match the place to go with what you would see there.

a) actor, b) ballerina, c) orchestra, d) plants, e) roller coaster, f) crafts, g) wild animals

1. zoo _____   **3.** botanical garden _____   **5.** craft fair _____   **7.** amusement park _____

2. ballet _____   **4.** theater _____   **6.** concert _____

10.6 Cross out the instrument that doesn't belong in the group.

Strings	Woodwind	Brass
piano	flute	trombone
guitar	clarinet	saxophone
violin	saxophone	French horn
drum	recorder	trumpet
double bass	cymbal	tuba

11 ANIMALS

11.1 Circle the animals that are kept in a cage.

gerbil	tropical fish	cat
parakeet	hamster	dog
goldfish	guinea pig	kitten

11.2 Match the animal with the name of its baby. Write the matching letter on the line.

a. calf   b. foal   c. gosling   d. chick   e. piglet   f. lamb   g. kid

1. horse _____

2. goose _____

3. sheep _____

4. pig _____

5. cow _____

6. goat _____

11.3 Complete the names of the wild animals.

1. el_phant	**6.** _onkey
2. g_raffe	**7.** c_eetah
3. ze_ra	**8.** ll_ma
4. tige_	**9.** li_ard
5. ka_garoo	**10.** racco_n

11.4 Put the animals into the correct category.

chipmunk, shrimp, wasp, flamingo, skunk, mosquito, bass, eagle, ostrich, swan, trout, mole, walrus, bluejay, ant, lobster, groundhog, fly, dolphin, octopus, shark

birds	sea animals	insects	fish	small animals
_____	_____	_____	_____	_____
_____	_____	_____	_____	_____
_____	_____	_____	_____	_____
_____	_____	_____		_____
_____	_____			

EXERCISES

12 THE ENVIRONMENT

12.1 Write the weather for each of these places.

Example: In San Francisco, it is foggy.

1. In Washington D.C., it is_____

2. In Miami, it is_____

3. In Los Angeles, it is _____

4. In New York, it is _____

12.2 Find the words for the pictures in the word soup.

```
H  N  H  V  B  X  G  O  S  E  N  Y  M  U  Y
W  I  J  V  E  O  C  M  K  S  E  Y  E  B  M
E  X  L  I  A  L  I  A  O  L  N  I  A  A  W
L  K  N  L  C  P  L  N  L  U  J  I  D  J  C
D  L  Y  K  H  K  V  A  Z  H  N  P  O  P  R
K  A  A  T  S  X  V  G  Y  J  K  T  W  P  M
I  E  M  W  A  T  E  R  F  A  L  L  A  E  P
P  T  X  O  G  O  M  C  A  V  E  E  R  I  H
S  L  C  B  S  T  P  A  E  Q  F  M  V  T  N
W  X  T  R  H  L  T  R  E  E  G  I  F  A  M
Y  R  D  E  S  E  R  T  C  S  E  G  Y  P  B
I  B  D  U  H  Z  Z  P  F  N  H  P  I  O  N
G  U  W  S  J  O  R  O  L  Q  P  I  N  N  Q
H  K  F  D  H  C  J  E  V  T  U  X  S  D  B
H  Q  L  P  U  X  O  T  B  B  J  S  J  Y  T
```

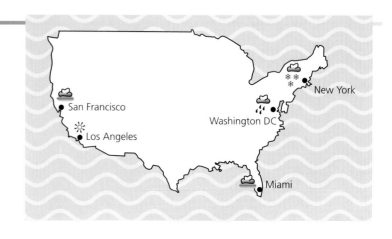

12.3 Write the names of the planets in the correct order from the nearest to the furthest from the sun.

Mercury	Saturn	Pluto
Earth	Venus	Neptune
Jupiter	Mars	Uranus

1. _____ **4.** _____ **7.** _____

2. _____ **5.** _____ **8.** _____

3. _____ **6.** _____ **9.** _____

1 NUMBERS, TIME, HOLIDAYS

1.1
1. first
2. second
3. third
4. fourth
5. fifth

1.2

Oval	Rectangle
egg	flag
watermelon	door

Circle	
clock	calculator
plate	
tire	
baseball	

1.3
Father's Day – June
Thanksgiving – November
Valentine's Day – February
Christmas – December
Memorial Day – May
Halloween – October
Independence Day – July

1.4
1. 7:30 a.m.
2. 2:00 p.m.
3. 4:00 p.m.
4. noon
5. 11 o'clock in the evening

2 PEOPLE

2.1
1. wake up
2. get up
3. take a shower
4. dry yourself
5. get dressed
6. go to work

2.2
1. Douglas
2. Michael
3. Male
4. Actor
5. 1106 Hollywood Drive, Los Angeles, CA
6. 98554
7. 994-9872
8. American
9. 09/25/1944
10. New Brunswick, New Jersey
11. Married
12. Catherine Zeta-Jones
13. 2 children

2.3
1. sister
2. father
3. aunt
4. grandmother
5. nephew
6. stepson
7. mother-in-law
8. half-sister
9. granddaughter
10. stepfather

2.4
1. single
2. married
3. widow
4. remarried
5. divorced

3 HOUSING

3.1
Kitchen
oven
microwave
spice rack
Bathroom
laundry basket
toilet
Dining Room
chandelier
napkin
Living Room
armchair
coffee table
sofa/couch
Bedroom
headboard
quilt
dresser

3.2
1. bedroom
2. dining room
3. bathroom
4. yard
5. bathroom
6. kitchen
7. yard
8. kitchen
9. bedroom

3.3
1. Bedroom/bathtub
2. Bathroom/quilt
3. Living room/razor
4. Yard/crib

3.4
1. fork
2. spoon
3. wine glass
4. plate
5. napkin
6. knife
7. tablespoon
8. salt
9. pepper
10. teaspoon

4 WORK

4.1
1. office
2. hospital
3. school
4. university
5. court
6. studio
7. bank
8. kitchen
9. restaurant

4.2
conduct a meeting
file papers
send a fax
sign a letter
photocopy a letter
send an e-mail

4.3
pencil holder 4
in box 8
paper clip 12
out box 9
white out™ 11
Rolodex 6
PC 1
tape 10
telephone 5
lamp 2
desk calendar 3
desk 7

5 THE BODY

5.1
This man has **short black** hair. He has **big** eyes and a **long** nose. He has **long** eyelashes and thick **eyebrows**. His mouth is **small** and his **ears** are small too. He has a **long** beard and a **mustache**.

5.2
1. to frown
2. to sing
3. to hug
4. to push
5. to pull
6. to sit
7. to talk
8. to wave
9. to cry
10. to shake hands

5.3
1c, 2d, 3a, 4e, 5b

5.4

Head/Face	Leg
nose	thigh
ears	hip
forehead	ankle
cheek	calf
mouth	knee
lips	kneecap

Arm/Hand	Body
wrist	waist
palm	stomach
elbow	back
fingers	
thumb	

6 FOOD

6.1
Hello, sir. What would you like to eat?
For an appetizer I would like **shrimp cocktail**.
And for the main course?
I would like **roast beef and a baked potato**.
Would you like dessert?
Yes. Can I have **apple pie** please?
And to drink?
I would like **bottled water**.

6.2

Meat	Drinks
chicken	orange juice
bacon	beer
ground beef	mineral water
pork chops	
liver	

Fish and seafood
shrimp
lobster
crab
Dry goods and condiments
pepper
oil
sugar
cereal
vinegar
salt
pasta
rice
cookies

6.3
Across
DOUGHNUT
SOUP
NAPKIN
HAMBURGER
Down
ICE CREAM
PIZZA
TACO
Diagonal
SODA
CHIPS

7 TRANSPORT

7.1
1. track
2. platform
3. luggage compartment

4. bus stop
5. timetable
6. passenger
7. engine
8. train station

7.2
1. gas cap
2. roof rack
3. side mirror
4. tire
5. bumper
6. trunk
7. door
8. exhaust pipe
9. hood
10. headlight

7.3
1. ticket
2. bellhop
3. baggage claim area
4. customs
5. suitcase
6. boarding pass
7. passport
8. luggage cart
Spells the word: t-e-r-m-i-n-a-l

7.4
Air
helicopter
jet plane
Land
sedan
hatchback
four-wheel drive
convertible
station wagon
Sea
yacht
cabin cruiser
rowboat
oil tanker
cruise ship
ferry

8 COMMUNITY
7.1
Fire station
fire hydrant
ladder
hose
smoke
fire extinguisher
Ambulance service
stretcher
drip
ambulance
oxygen mask
paramedic
Phone booth
coinslot

phonecard
receiver

8.2
1d, 2c, 3g, 4e, 5f, 6b, 7a

8.3
1. postmark
2. letter
3. zip code
4. address
5. envelope
6. postcard
7. stamp

9 SPORTS
9.1
Water sports
surfing
sailing
rowing
diving
Individual sports
golf
tennis
Winter sports
speed skating
downhill skiing
figure skating
Team sports
football
basketball
baseball

9.2
Across
MITT
BASE
UMPIRE
OUTFIELD
Down
STADIUM
PITCHER
INFIELD
Diagonal
CATCHER

9.3
2. No, they don't.
3. Yes, they do.
4. No, they don't.
5. No, they don't.
6. No, they don't.
7. Yes they do.
8. Yes they do.
9. No, they don't.
10. No, they don't.

10 ENTERTAINMENT
10.1
photography/camera
knitting/knitting needles
pottery/potter's wheel

painting/brush
astronomy/telescope
bird-watching/binoculars

10.2
Things you take …
surfboard, float, beach towel,
bucket, swimsuit, cooler, shovel
sunglasses
Things you find …
pier, sea, seashell, wave

10.3
1. backpack
2. path
3. fisherman
4. signpost
5. campsite
6. hiking
7. sleeping bag
Spells the word:
c-a-m-p-i-n-g

10.4
1. chess
2. dice
3. computer games
4. backgammon
5. checkers
6. cards

10.5
1g, 2b, 3d, 4a, 5f, 6c, 7e

10.6
Strings – drum
Woodwind- cymbal
Brass- saxophone

11 ANIMALS
11.1
Animals that are kept in a cage:
gerbil
parakeet
hamster
guinea pig

11.2
1b, 2c, 3f, 4e, 5a, 6g

11.3
1. elephant
2. giraffe
3. zebra
4. tiger
5. kangaroo
6. monkey
7. cheetah
8. llama
9. lizard
10. raccoon

11.4
birds
flamingo
eagle

ostrich
swan
bluejay
sea animals
shrimp
walrus
lobster
dolphin
octopus
insects
wasp
mosquito
ant
fly
fish
bass
trout
shark
small animals
chipmunk
skunk
mole
groundhog

12 ENVIRONMENT
12.1
1. In Washington D.C., it is cloudy and rainy.
2. In Miami, it is cloudy.
3. In Los Angeles, it is sunny.
4. In New York, it is cloudy and snowy.

12.2
Across
WATERFALL (9)
CAVE (2)
DESERT (4)
TREE (1)
Down
BEACH (10)
MEADOW (5)
POND (11)
Diagonal
HILL (12)
DAM (3)
LAKE (8)
MOUNTAIN (7)
PEAK (6)
VALLEY (13)

12.3
1. Mercury
2. Venus
3. Earth
4. Mars
5. Jupiter
6. Saturn
7. Uranus
8. Neptune
9. Pluto

Ace Photography **107** 12.

AP/Wide World **6** 3, 5; **9** 5, 6; **27** 19; **36** 4–6; **71** 8, 14–15; **76** 4; **81** 11.

Ascension © 2002 **9** 1–4; **12** 1–21; **37** 1–37; **39** 21–22; **40** 2–4, 6–11, 13–14, 17–18, 21; **41** 1; **43** 16; **44** 1, 13, 15; **45** 21, 25, 33; **49** 7; **52** 21–23; **71** 1–2, 4–7, 12–13; **72** 1–4, 6, 14–17, 21–24; **73** 1–28; **74** 1–7, 14–15; **75** 4; **76** 1, 7–8, 11–12, 16–17; **78** 10, 12, 20–21; **79** 3, 5; **80** 1–5, 7, 13–20; **81** 1, 9–10, 13–14; **82** 1; **85** 6, 24; **90** 22–24; **92** 8–22; **111** 3; **112** 3, 9; **113** 1–2, 7–8, 25–26; **115** 1.

Addenbrookes Hospital **44** 11; **46** 17.

Allsport **4** 1–5; **87** 7–18; **88** 1–5, 7, 8, 17, 23, 24; **89** 3–5, 17–19; 90 4, 7–11, 12, 13, 28–31; **91** 3–7, 10., 11, 16–18, 19–21, 22, 23; **97** 22–24.

The Anthony Blake Photo Library Ltd **14** 3–6; **61** 22, 23; **62** 31–36; **63** 9, 10, 11, 15, 16; **65** 1–6, 8–10, 20, 21–26, 27, 28; **66** 1, 2, 4–7, 10–12, 14, 15, 19, 20, 21, 22; **67** 5, 14; **70** 6–8.

Mark Wagner – Aviation Images **77** 35.

BAA Picture Library **76** 19, 20; **77** 37–39, 44–48.

Gareth Bowden **14** 11–15, 18; **15** 1, 20–23, 27–29; **17** 20, 21, 23, 24; **19** 6, 14–18, 20–23; **20** 4–6; 21 10–12, 20; **22** 1–4, 8, 14; **23** 1, 3–11, 13, 15, 16; **25** 7, 9, 10, 12; **29** 14; **36** 1, 3–22, 24–26; **35** 9–11, 15; **39** 13, 19, 20; **40** 1, 5, 12, 15, 19, 20; **41** 2–15, 19; **42** 1, 3–22, 24–26; **45** 20, 29–31, 36, 37; **49** 4, 5; **50** 2–5, 7; **51** 1–6, 9, 10, 14–21; **52** 2, 3, 6, 9, 10, 12–15, 17–18; **57** 2, 5, 6; **60** 7–11, 14; **62** 17–20; **74** 10–13; **83** 15, 22, 26; **89** 20; **92** 2–4; **94** 13; **97** 18, 20; **109** 14; **110** 2; **113** 17, 18.

BusinessWire **79** 5.

Corbis **6** 2 (© Reed Kaestner), 7 (© Bettmann); **27** 10, 14; **29** 6; **34** 7; **47** 1; **84** 2, 7–9, 12; **86** 11, 12 (© Kevin Flemming), 13–16 (Chris Trotman ©Duromo/CORBIS); **92** 6; **93** 10, 11 (©Robbie Jack); **94** 12, 27; **99** 11, 12 (©Dave G. Houser).

Corel Picture Library **6** 7; **9** 12, 13; **25** 15, 18; **28** 12; **29** 16; **39** 3–4, 14; **56** 2, 5, 9–14, 18; **57** 4, 8; **59** 2, 11, 17; **62** 16, 24; **67** 11–13; **75** 1, 5–6, 8–12, 15–18; **77** 43; **80** 6, 12; **85** 7–14, 18–19; **86** 5, 9–10; **88** 18; **89** 1, 6–10; **90** 16–18, 19–21; **91** 1, 8–9, 12–15; **92** 1, 5; **93** 13, 18–19; **98** 2–3; **99** 9, 13–15; **102** 31–32; **103** 27–28; **104** 4; **105** 8, 14, 18, 20, 24–25; **106** 18; **113** 29–30.

Digital Stock **59** 5.

DIY Photo Library **32** 7, 17, 18.

Dorling Kindersley **14** 10; **15** 4, 5, 10, 24, 30; **17** 22; **22** 15–17, 19, 20; **23** 14, 19, 22; **34** 14, 15; **36** 1, 3; **38** 1–7; **39** 1, 2, 5–12, 16, 17, 18, 23, 24; **46** 18; **47** 20, 21; **52** 1; **54** 17; **55** 8, 9, 12–21, 24, 29, 31, 32; **58** 11, 12; **61** 27; **62** 15, 27, 29; **65** 4; **66** 18; **69** 1–4, 6–13, 16–21, 23–26; **72** 9; **77** 28, 34, 36; **78** 7, 8, 14, 15; **85** 16, 17; **89** 6–10, 21, 22; **93** 6–8, 23–26; **94** 7–9, 11, 14, 16, 23, 24; 95 2–9; **96** 1–22, 24–28; **97** 13; **98** 11–13; **99** 7; **102** 11, 12; **106** 4, 8, 17, 19, 25, 26, 28; **107** 4; **109** 1–12; **110** 1, 19, 20; **111** Photographer, 20, 21.

Fashion Wire Daily **49** 11, 20–21; **50** 19–20.

Fresno Bee **84** 4.

Getty Images, © Taxi **10** 1–3, 5–14; **11** 15–22. ImageWorks **27** 11 (© Frank Pedrick), 13 (© Jack Kurtz); **28** 7 (© Rhoda Sidney); **29** 2 (© Bob Daemmrich), 4 (© Jonathan Nouvok), 5 (© Tannen Maury); **31** 4, 7 (© Jim Pickerell), 5–6 (© Bill Bachman); **33** 1–2 (© Dion Ogust); **36** 2 (© Rhoda Sidney); **46** 8 (© Frozen Images), 11 (© David Grossman), 14 (© Bob Daemmrich), 16 (© John Griffin); **47** 3–5 (IW Network); **58** 22 (© Tony Aruza); **59** 1 (© Syracuse Newspapers/Dick Blume), 3 (© DPA/MAK), 15 (© Bob Mahoney), 16 (© James Marshall); **85** 1 (© Rhonda Sidney); **91** 2 (© Syracuse Newspapers/Logan Wallace); **111** 19 (© Jonathan Nouvok).

Indianapolis Star **115** 4.

Joel Gordon © 2002 **85** 2.

Charlie Gray **94** 1, 2.

Hart McLeod **4** 6–48; **5** 1–24; **6** A, B; **7** 6–22, 8 Map; **18** 20; 27 16; **24** 1–4, 6–12, 15, 16; **34** 8, 11, 12, 20; **40** 16; **60** 18; **62** 28; **66** 3; **81** 6, 7; **90** 25–27; **107** 17–22; **108** 12; **109** 15–20; **115** 14–16.

J C Bamford Excavators Ltd (JCB) **34** 18.

McDonald's Graphic Services **67** 4, 6.

NASCAR **56** 8.

National Sporting Goods **57** 9.

Philips **43** 21

PhotoDisc **6** 10; **27** 5; **28** 9–10, 13; **29** 3, 7, 18; **30** 17–18; **31** 3; **46** 2–4, 7; **47** 6, 12; **48** 1–8, 15, 18, 25; **50** 15–18; **58** 17; **61** 9; **62** 14; **86** 6–8, 13–21; **97** 7; **100** 10, 17; PhotoEdit, all rights reserved. **6** 10 (© David Young–Wolff); **9** 9, 10 (© Robert Brenner); **20** 1–2 (© Laura Dwight), 17 (© Robert Brenner), 19 (© Spencer Grant), 20 (© Patrick Olear); **21** 8 (© Robert Brenner); **23** 17, 20 (© David Young–Wolff); **25** 1 (© Mary Kate Denney), 2 (© Tony Freeman), 6, 13, 19 (© Michael Newman), 8 (© Robert Brenner), 14 (© Myrleen Ferguson Cate), 17 (© David Young–Wolff); **29** 8, 10 (© Bill Bachmann); **31** 1 (© Susan Van Etten); **47** 1 (© Patrick Olear); **58** 18 (© Robert Brenner); **59** 4 (© David Young–Wolff), 14 (© Mary Kate Denny); **76** 18 (© Phil McCarten); **93** 1, 4–5 (© Tony Freeman); **94** 19 (© David Young–Wolff).

PictureQuest **29** 9 (© Jim Pickerell/Stock Connection); **33** 6 (© Benelux Press, b.v./eStock Photography), 13–14 (© Ryan McVay/PhotoDisc); **43** 15 (© Creasource/Series); **77** 22–27 (© Pictor International Ltd.); **79** 1, 7–9 (© Jim Pickerell/Stock Connection); **94** 4–5 (© Everett C. Johnson/e–Stock Photography).

The Photographers Library 90 5, 6; 107 13.

Pictor **44** 8, 17–19; **88** 6; **99** 2–4; **105** 1, 2.

Planet Earth Pictures **78** 9; **101** 1–4, 7–12, 17, 18; **102** 23, 27, 28, 30; **103** 7, 9, 11, 13–15, 18, 22–26; **104** 1, 3, 5–11, 14–24, 26–30; **105** 3–7, 9, 11, 15–17, 19, 21; **106** 6, 7, 11–16, 21–23, 29; **108** 13–16, 22–30.

PRNewswire **6** 1; **9** 16; **10** 4; **11** 23; **21** 9; **24** 15; **35** 12; **46** 5; **47** 17; **49** 6, 10, 12–13, 15; **50** 6; **58** 13; **59** 3 (logos), 10; **72** 5, 10; **74** 9; **84** 3, 10, 14; **86** 1–4, 22–24; **88** 15–16, 19–22; **89** 11–12; **93** 14, 16–17, 20–22; **94** 21–22; **98** 7–8; **99** 6; **110** 4–9.

Poppertfoto **84** 7.

Royal Flyer Inc. © 2002 all rights reserved **57** 7.

Stock, Boston **13** E (Milton Feinberg).

Sandra Small Photography **15** 7, 11; **16** 10–18, 20–23; **17** 1–6, 9–16; **18** 1–19, 21–22; **19** 1–5, 7–12, 19; **20** 3, 9, 11–15, 18; **43** 1–9; 44 3–4, 6–10, 12, 14, 16; **45** 28–30, 35; **49** 1–3; **50** 1, 8–14; **51** 7–8, 11–13; **54** 1–7, 10–14, 24–30; **58** 1–9; **60** 1–6, 15–18, 20–21; **61** 1–8; **62** 1–13,

21–23, 25–26; **63** 12–14, 17–19, 21–22; **64** 1–26; **65** 14–15, 29–34; **66** 26–28; **67** 3, 7–10; **68** 1–5, 7–8, 11–17; **70** 2–5, 9–10, 12–13, 19; **79** 6, 10–12, 17–23; **82** 2–11; **83** 3–5, 7–8, 12–14, 17–18, 20–21, 22–29; **94** 3; **111** 1–2, 4–8; **113** 5–6, 15–16, 21–22, 27–28; **114** 3–8, 13–14; **115** 2–3, 7–13, 17–18.

R & S Greenhill **6** 6, 8.

Reeve Photography **14** 16; **15** 2, 3, 6, 8, 9, 12–16, 19, 25, 26; **16** 9; 17 7, 8, 17–19; **19** 13; 20 1, 8, 10; **21** 1, 2, 13, 18, 19; 23 2; **26** 7; **30** 11–13, 15, 16, 19; **32** 1–6, 8–13, 15, 16, 19–24; **33** 9, 10; **34** 23–25; **35** 16; **38** 23–29; **43** 7, 10–14, 17–20, 22–25; **45** 22, 26, 34; **46** 1; **47** 22; **48** 19–22; **53** 1–23; **54** 4, 5, 20–23; **55** 1–7, 10, 11, 22, 23, 25–28, 30; **57** 10, 11, 14, 16–18, 20–24; **58** 10; **59** 11; **61** 10–21, 24–26; **63** 20; **65** 11–13, 34; **66** 23–25, 29; **68** 9, 10, 20–25; **69** 5, 14; **70** 1, 11; **82** 22–24; **83** 16; **88** 9; **92** 7; **94** 18; **95** 1; **96** 23; **97** 5, 8, 9; **98** 6; **109** 13, 14; **110** 3, 10; **111** 10, 13, 14, 16–18, 22, 23; **112** 1, 2, 4–8, 10; **113** 3, 4, 9–14, 17, 18, 23, 24; **114** 9, 10; **115** 5, 6.

RSPCA Photolibrary **100** 1, 3, 4, 6, 7, 11–14; **101** 5, 14, 16, 20, 21; **102** 1–5, 13, 34; **103** 21; **104** 2; **105** 2.

Science Photo Library **38** 11, 12 (©Geoff Tompkinson), 16–119 (© Martin Dohrn).

Six Continents Hotels **35** 1–3, 13–14, 17–19.

Corbis Stockmarket **6** 4, 9; **25** 4; **33** 7, 8; **54** 18, 19; **58** 19, 20; **84** 5; **94** 25, 26; **107** 6, 9, 10, 14.

Susan G. Holtz/Image & Film Research © 2002 **13** 1–23; **14** 1–2, 7–9, 17; **15** 17; **16** 1–8, 19, 24–26; **20** 16; **21** 3–7, 14–17, 21; **22** 9–13; **24** 5; **25** 3, 5, 16; **27** 7, 17–18; **28** 11; **30** 1–9, 14, 20–21, 23; **31** 2, 8, 10; **33** 4–5, 10; **34** 13, 19; **35** 4–6; **37** 7–17; **41** 16; **42** 2; **48** 9; **49** 4, 16–19; **52** 5; **54** 15–16; **56** 3–4, 6, 15–16, 20–22; **57** 1, 3, 12–13, 15, 25; **59** 13, 18; **60** 12, 19; **63** 1–8, B; **64** 29; **65** 17–18; **66** 8–9, 13, 16–17; **67** 1–2; **68** 18–19; **69** 22; **70** 14–18; **71** 9–10, 16–19; **72** 7–8, 11–13, 18–19; **73** 8; **74** 8; **75** 2–3, 7, 13–14; **76** 15; **77** 40–42; **78** 5; **79** 2, 13–16; **80** 8–11, 21; **81** 12; **82** 12–21; **84** 6, 15; **85** 3–4, 20–23, 25; **89** 15–16; **97** 1, 3–4, 6, 10–12, 14–16, 21; **98** 9–10, 14–19; **99** 5, 8, 10; **100** 8, 9; **110** 1, 11–18; **111** 9, 24; **113** 19–20, 31–32; **114** 1–2, 11–12, 15–16.

Tony Stone **59** 9.

Telegraph Colour Library **9** 7, 8, 11, 14, 15; **22** 18; **25** 11, 20; **26** 4–6; **27** 1–4, 6, 8, 9, 12; **28** 1–6, 8; 29 11–13, 15, 17; **33** 3, 11, 12, 15, 16; **34** 1–6, 9, 10, 16, 17; **39** 15; **42** 23; **44** 2; **46** 12, 13; **47** 8–11; **48** 17, 24; **58** 14–16, 21; **75** 1; **76** 8–10, 13; **77** 30–33; **78** 3, 4, 6, 11, 13, 16–19; **81** 2, 3; **84** 1, 11, 13; **85** 15; **87** 1–6; **89** 2, 13, 14, 23–25; **90** 1–3, 14, 15; **93** 2, 3; **94** 10; **97** 17; **98** 1, 4, 5; **99** 2; **100** 11, 12, 18–21; **101** 6, 16, 17, 22, 23; **102** 6–10, 14–22, 24–26, 29, 33, 35; **103** 1–5, 10, 12, 16, 17, 19, 20; **104** 12, 25; **106** 1–3, 5, 9, 10, 20; **107** 1–3, 5, 7, 8, 11, 16, 15; **108** 1–11, 17–21.

Telegraph Herald **27** 15.

The Decatur Daily **94** 17.

The Plain Dealer **93** 15.

USGC Digital **78** 2.

U.S. Coast Guard, AMT1, Wes Fleming **78** 1.

The Wellcome Trust **38** 8–10; **44** 5, 20; **45** 23, 24, 27, 28, 32, 35, 38; **46** 6, 9, 10; **47** 13–15; **48** 10–14, 16, 23.

ACKNOWLEDGEMENTS

Director
Della Summers

Editorial Director
Adam Gadsby

Senior Publisher
Laurence Delacroix

Editor
Jennifer Sagala

ELT Consultant and photobrief
Tamara Colloff-Bennett

Design and photography
Hart McLeod and Susan G. Holtz

Production
Clive McKeough

Conversation activities
Liz Sharman

Exercises
Russell Stannard

Pronunciation Editor
Rebecca Dauer

Pearson Education Limited
Edinburgh Gate
Harlow
Essex CM20 2JE
England
and Associated Companies throughout the world

Visit our website: http://www.longman.com/dictionaries

© Pearson Education Limited 2003, 2005
All rights reserved; no part of this publication may be reproduced, stored in a retrieval system,
or transmitted in any form or by any means, electronic, mechanical, photocopying, recording
or otherwise, without the prior written permission of the Publishers.

First edition 2003
Second edition 2005
Sixth impression 2010

Words that the editors have reason to believe constitute trademarks have been described as such. However, neither the presence nor the absence of such a description should be regarded as affecting the legal status of any trademark.

ISBN 978-1-4058-2796-6 (paper + audio CDs)

British Library Cataloguing-in-Publication Data
A catalogue record for this book is available from the British Library.

Library of Congress Cataloging-in-Publication Data
A catalog record for this book has been applied for.

Set in Frutiger by Hart McLeod, Cambridge
Printed in China GCC/06

PRONUNCIATION TABLE

Symbol Consonants	Keyword	Symbol Vowels	Keyword
p	**p**ack	e	b**e**d
b	**b**ack	æ	b**a**d
t	**t**ie	i	k**ee**per
d	**d**ie	ɑ	**fa**ther
k	**c**lass	ɔ	**ca**ller
g	**g**lass	ʊ	p**u**t
tʃ	**ch**urch	u	grad**u**al
dʒ	ju**dg**e	ʌ	**c**ut
f	**f**ew	ɚ	b**ir**d
v	**v**iew	ə	ban**a**na
θ	**th**row	eɪ	m**a**ke
ð	**th**ough	aɪ	b**i**te
s	**s**oon	ɔɪ	b**oy**
z	**z**oo	aʊ	n**ow**
ʃ	**sh**oe	oʊ	b**oa**t
ʒ	mea**s**ure	ɪr	**h**ere
m	su**m**	er	h**air**
n	su**n**	ʊr	p**oor**
ŋ	su**ng**	eɪɚ	pl**ayer**
h	**h**ot	aɪɚ	t**ire**
l	**l**ot	ɔɪɚ	empl**oyer**
r	**r**od	aʊɚ	fl**ower**
j	**y**et	oʊɚ	l**ower**
w	**w**et		
t̮	bu**tt**er	/ˈ/ shows main stress	
t˺	bu**tt**on	/ˌ/ shows secondary stress	